LARAMIE, WYOMING

IN MEMORY OF

Eric Lindahl

PRESENTED BY

A Friend

ICE PALACES

ICE PALACES

Fred Anderes
and Ann Agranoff

Abbeville Press • Publishers • New York

For Bess and Irving Agranoff

FRONT COVER: Ice palace, Sapporo, 1975

FRONTISPIECE: Ice palace, Sapporo, 1978

ACKNOWLEDGMENTS:

We would like to thank the following people for their help and support: Normal Ball, Faith Baum, Ken Elder, Anthony Gow, Mayumi Kurihara, David Lampe, Bob Olsen, Raymond Plourde, Frederick Roll, Hitoshi Shirano, Raymond St. Laurent, Hachiro Takahashi, and Albert Wuori.

This project was supported, in part, by a grant from the National Endowment for the Arts in Washington, D.C., a Federal agency.

Editor: Walton Rawls   Designer: Robin Fox

Library of Congress Cataloging in Publication Data
Anderes, Fred.
  Ice palaces.
  Bibliography: p. 129
  Includes index.
  1. Ice palaces I. Agranoff, Ann.   II. Title.
NA6890.A52 1983   730   83-6061
ISBN 0-89659-391-6
ISBN 0-89659-393-2 (pbk.)

Contents

Eyewitnesses agree that ice palaces are extraordinary; the wonder of their fabric gives ice palaces a feeling of magic. Fragile and massive, transparent and solid, colorful and dazzling white, ice shimmers with contradictions by its very nature. (St. Paul, 1889 and 1890)

Introduction

A FAIRY-TALE castle appears. Massive yet delicate, thick yet translucent, shifting in color from shadowy blue to warm rose and gold, its highlights sparkling like the facets of a giant jewel, spacious and elegant yet not the exclusive province of a nobility, it reigns briefly over an urban skyline and then vanishes, as completely as a dewdrop in the sun. While such fanciful structures as this may not seem, at first, to make economic sense, they have been built and they continue to be built, not from glass or concrete, stone or steel, but, magically, from snow and ice.

Ice palaces were first constructed in Russia in the eighteenth century. They reached their peak of development over a hundred years later in the United States and Canada, in the cities of Montreal, St. Paul, Quebec, Ottawa, and Leadville. Their purpose was always to delight and entertain, and usually to serve as the focus of a winter carnival. We hope this book will bring these beautiful and imaginative but sadly forgotten structures the attention they deserve.

Ice palaces began in Russia in the eighteenth century, and reached their peak of development more than a hundred years later. The first ice palace, shown here, was a honeymoon suite for a reluctant couple. The bride and groom traveled from church to ice palace on elephant-back, followed by a bizarre procession. (St. Petersburg, 1740)

Ice palaces were impressive feats of engineering. At a height of 140 feet, the 1887 St. Paul castle topped every other building in the city. FACING

Ice palaces were always lit up at night. Against the dark sky, they glowed like giant alabaster lanterns or glittered like huge piles of diamonds. Often, colored glass or gelatin lenses added bits of rainbow to their sparkle. (Montreal, 1889) ABOVE

Those of us who have never seen an ice palace must rely on the accounts of eyewitnesses for our vision. On one thing, these accounts all agree—the castles were extraordinary:

The delightful material gave a new, fantastic beauty to every feature, sometimes white and sometimes clear green—dark and opaque where the shadows fell, and almost transparent in the sun. No dream castle of jasper or beryl or chrysoprase could be more beautiful than these wonderful buildings of ice.[1]

The palaces were always lit at night:

The ice palace is lit up by the electric light, the effect of which is heightened by the myriad facets of the ice blocks through which it shines, so that from a distance the building looks like a great heap of jewels dropped upon a sheet of crystal.[2]

In the bright light of the Northern sun; beneath the soft silvery sheen of the moon; or, when illuminated by dazzling fires of varied hues, struggling with the intense white light of the electrics, the effort is incomparably grand and impressive.[3]

Creativity found ample room to play in the castles:

Loftier and covering a larger area, it was yet more boldly fantastic in design, a wilderness of tower and turret, battlement and pinnacle, tall arch and flying buttress.[4]

The palaces were impressive feats of engineering. The tower of the 1887 St. Paul castle reached a height of fourteen stories,

Ice palaces were the settings for dramatic mock battles, fought with fireworks. Rockets rose in flights of color from every turret. Whirling wheels of scarlet and gold flamed on the battlements. (St. Paul, 1888)

overshadowing every other building in the city.

These structures were built with the intention of lasting probably three months at most, and yet rivaled the most prominent buildings in the world in style, form, and engineering.[5]

Almost every castle was the setting for a mock battle known as ''the storming of the ice palace,'' climaxed by a dramatic display of fireworks.

The building, white and ghost-like before, breaks suddenly ablaze with purple and rose. From every window Roman Candles answer those from without. From every turret rockets rise in flights of brilliant color.

The battlements are aflame with whirling wheels of scarlet and gold.[6]

The delicate loveliness of the palaces inspired flights of fancy:

There is a popular fallacy to the effect that the Ice Palace is built; built by mere men who saw out the blocks of ice with saws, heave them with ice-tongs and derricks into place and lay them as the commonplace bricklayer lays brick. But this is all nonsense . . .

Look at it! Look at the light vaulting arches and stately turrets. Massive it stands, but as light as a castle of the clouds. Mysteriously beautiful and dim in its semi-translucency, and glittering from a thousand diamond facets where the winter sun strikes its angles. All the gods of Asgard never built anything more lovely. Alph, the sacred river, flowed by no structure more majestically fairy-like.

That thing built by men? Nonsense! It rose as the walls of Athens rose, to the sound of the music of gods.[7]

The palaces left deep impressions on those who saw them:

The bright memory will linger long after the hot sun of summer has dissolved the mystic mansion, and the released liquid has flowed away to the sunny South where it can never more be imprisoned in [the] donjon tower of [an] Ice Palace.[8]

It is as if the Palaces have a soul, for everyone I've met, from people on the bus to the men in the city architect's office, speaks of the Palaces as if they will again appear.[9]

One writer describes ''a weird and mystic palace of fairy fancy in a world of crystal gloom,'' highlighted by ''scintillating rays of rainbow-tinted hues.'' He concludes:

It was a dream of beauty which can never fade from the memory of one who gazed upon its pure, transparent loveliness.[10]

After looking at hundreds of pictures of ice palaces and their attendant festivities, one can only be filled with admiration for their grace and daring. Perhaps you, too, after gazing at these crystal visions, will yearn for the days when they were not a rarity, and hope that this almost lost art will someday be widely revived.

1
Villa
on the Neva

Imperial mistress of fur-clad Russ,
Thy most magnificent and mighty freak,
The wonder of the North. No forest fell
When thou didst build. No quarry sent its stores
To enrich thy walls. But thou didst hew the floods
And make thy marble of the glassy wave.
Ice upon ice, thy well-adjusted parts
Were soon conjoined, nor other cement asked
Than water interfused to make them one.

WILLIAM COWPER, 1731-1800, "*The Task*"

The first well-documented ice palace was built as the setting for a monstrous joke. On the frozen River Neva, in the winter of 1739-40, a shivering bride and groom spent their wedding night in a building of ice. The palace was designed by the architect Eropkin, conceived by the imperial adviser Volynski, and commissioned by the Empress Anna Ivanovna.

George William Krafft, the first historian of the 1740 ice palace, writes that "the Empress Anna of glorious memory . . . never refused the ingenious projects of her subjects, even when they only pertained to entertainment."[1]

Although Anna funded the ice palace generously, her ghost surely is marching in step with the eccentric and brutal parade of Russian czars. A very tall, fat woman, she devoted herself to shooting and riding. She kept loaded guns at the windows of her residence and used them to bring down birds that flew by.

Like her uncle, Peter the Great, Anna had a malicious sense of humor. She was entertained by a troupe of dwarfs, deformed people, and idiots. Four of her six court jesters were members of ancient noble families that she delighted in humiliating. For her pleasure, they would dress up and fight each other until their blood flowed. When one of these jesters, Prince Mikhail Golitsyn, infuriated Anna by converting to Roman Catholicism, she forced him to sit on a basket of eggs and cackle until they hatched.[2]

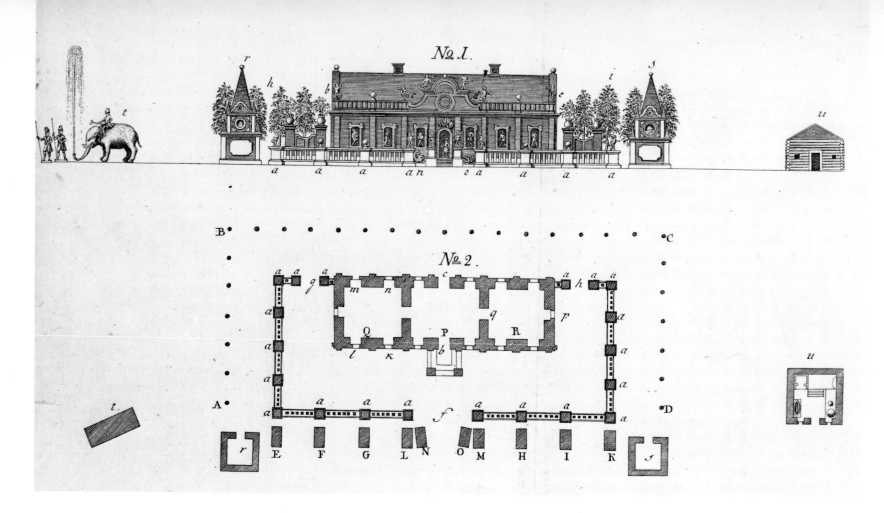

Empress Anna had the first ice palace built as the setting for a monstrous joke. In the bitterly cold winter of 1740, she forced the out-of-favor Prince Mikhail Golitsyn to marry a servant and honeymoon in a frozen villa on the Neva. (Elevation and floor plan)

In the autumn of 1739, shortly before she undertook the exquisite project that guaranteed her a place in architectural history, Anna ordered two series of bloody political executions. The noble Dolgoruki family had been exiled to Siberia at the time of her accession. The empress now recalled Prince Sergei Dolgoruki and entrusted him with a special mission, but changed her mind at the last minute and brought him and all of his relatives to trial instead. "Found guilty of concocted charges of treason, Prince Sergei was beheaded, princes Vasili and Ivan broken on the wheel, while two other members of the family were drawn and quartered."[3]

Then in November, 1739, in a Ukrainian village, a man proclaimed himself the tsarevich Alexis. This prince actually had been killed in 1718, at the order of his father, Peter the Great. However, three soldiers and the village priest believed the imposter and held a mass for him. When Anna learned of the affair, she acted swiftly and brutally. She had the pretender impaled alive, and the priest and the three soldiers almost as gruesomely exterminated. "However, the Empress, 'in her clemency,' pardoned the peasants and permitted them to settle elsewhere after their village was razed to the ground."[4]

As winter succeeded fall, temperatures plummeted. The winter of 1739-40 was one of the coldest in history. The Seine, the Rhine, the Danube, and the Thames were frozen solid for many months. "That year the Duc de Saint Simon complained that at Versailles, even in the few heated rooms, the cold was so extreme that it burst bottles of brandy; and when he dined in the Duc de Villeroi's little bedroom, next to his kitchen, where there was a big fire, the wine froze in the drinking glasses." In the Ukraine, birds fell dead from the sky as they tried to fly south.[5]

In Lubeck, Germany, a Lieutenant Meynerts built a bastion, defended by five cannons and a soldier, all of ice. Within the structure lay his masterpiece, an ice lion seven feet long.[6]

In St. Petersburg, to distract the people from the bitter cold and from the recent executions, Empress Anna built her ice palace as the stage for a wedding. The proceedings, which few modern readers will find comic, afforded Anna and her subjects considerable amusement. Once again, the butt was Prince Mikhail Golitsyn. Anna forced the recently widowed prince to marry one of her servants, a Kalmuck woman of exceptional ugliness, nicknamed *Buzhenina* after the Empress's favorite dish of roast pork with spiced vinegar and onion sauce.

After the church ceremony, the bride and groom, swathed in furs, seated in an iron cage fastened to the back of an elephant, headed an elaborate procession. Anna recruited the other participants in the parade, one hundred or more couples, from her various provinces. Lapps, Finns, Khirgiz, Bashkirs, and others, attired in their national costumes, traveled on horse or camel-back, or in sledges drawn by such unlikely animals as wolves and pigs. The celebration's climax was the bedding down of the bridal couple in an ice bed; guards posted outside made sure that they spent the whole night in the frozen mansion.

The married pair survived their ordeal. Buzhenina eventually bore her husband two sons, one of whom continued the family line. "After her death Prince Mikhail remarried for the fourth time, begat three daughters, and lived to the age of 89."[7]

Despite what we now consider its shameful use, this early ice palace was a true work of art: Its architect, Eropkin, had translated Palladio into Russian and created a sort of Palladian villa in ice. Eropkin and Volynski, who suggested the idea of an ice palace, had both been condemned to death as traitors by June 1740. When it became unsafe to mention their names, credit for their contributions to the palace was transferred to Alexis Tatishchev.

The contemporary engravings, which are reproduced here, give an idea of the villa's form, but to comprehend its spirit one must remember that its substance was transparent. The builders selected the clearest ice from the frozen Neva. The chosen material was carefully measured with compass and ruler, cut into blocks and set in place by cranes. Freezing water joined the blocks so smoothly that they appeared to be one piece. Krafft wrote in 1741 that the building was "infinitely more beautiful than if it had been constructed of the finest marble. The transparency and bluish tone of the ice gave it the look of some precious stone."[8]

The ice villa that rose up on the River Neva, between the Admiralty and the Winter Palace, was 56 feet long, 17½ feet wide, and over 21 feet high. It contained three rooms: a hall, a bedroom, and a drawing room. What it lacked in size, compared to later palaces, it made up for in exquisite craftsmanship. A low ice balustrade, topped at intervals with balls of ice, surrounded the house. Outside the balustrade stood twenty-nine trees, inhabited by birds. Both flora and fauna were sculpted from ice and painted in natural colors. Although most of the palace was left transparent, the pillars, doors, and window frames were painted to simulate green marble. The panes of the windows were made of the thinnest possible ice. The front of the palace held six niches containing ice statues, and an elaborate frontispiece set off the entrance.

Every detail of the palace, down to the pillows on the bed and the dishes on the table, was made of ice. Such superb ice craftsmanship probably has never been equaled. The architect Eropkin, who designed the palace, was later condemned to death. FACING

Ice dolphins sprayed jets of water. The ice cannon often were actually fired—to the amazement of visitors. The elaborate ice palace that these details adorned derived, ultimately, from the simple ice booths that the Russians built to celebrate Maslenitza, *their equivalent of carnival.* BELOW

Two dolphins, two mortars, and six cannons, all carved from ice, guarded the building. Flanking the balustrade were two ice spires, "inside which hung large, octagonal paper lanterns painted with strange, perhaps obscene figures. At night invisible hands rotated the candlelit lanterns so the populace could view all the pictures."[9]

At the opposite edges of the installation stood a traditional Russian bathhouse and a life-size elephant fountain. Although cannons, bathhouse, and fountain were all made of ice, all were actually used. The cannons were frequently loaded—one-quarter of a pound of gunpowder was needed for each shot—and fired, much to the delight of the admiring public. The bathhouse, built

of ice "logs," was sometimes heated and occupied; the ice elephant fountain spouted a 24-foot jet of water. The only nonglacial structure was a wooden picket fence erected around the whole exhibit to control the crowds.

The workmen had applied their most minute and exquisite craftsmanship to the interior of the palace. Everything was carved of ice, except for sets of real playing cards and counters frozen onto the surface of the drawing room table. This table also held a clock, made of ice clear enough to reveal its works. "Ice benches with ball feet faced each other from opposite walls. On the shelves of a gracefully carved corner cupboard ice replicas of all sorts of tempting dishes were set out, colored in their natural tints, along with a tea service, goblets, and glasses."[10]

The bedroom focused on a "large, elaborately curtained bed, furnished with a feather mattress, a quilt, and two pillows, a nightcap laid out on each—everything skillfully carved in ice."[11] Next to the bed stood a little table; a low stool held two pairs of slippers. Facing the dressing table, laden with boxes, bottles, and a pair of candlesticks, hung a prettily carved mirror. Opposite the bed was a fireplace. On special occasions, the ice logs in the fireplace and the ice candles on the dressing table were set aflame by dousing them with petroleum.

Two other Russian ice palaces are referred to by Krafft and North American winter carnival literature. According to Krafft, a fortress of snow and ice was built on the River Neva about 1734, also during Anna's reign. In a sham battle, it was attacked and defended according to all the rules of war, and finally taken, "sword in hand." This military display was probably the first example of what later festivals called "the storming of the ice palace." The St. Paul Winter Carnival souvenir brochure of 1886 refers to an ice palace "of much greater proportions" built on the Neva by Empress Elizabeth in 1754.

Although the 1740 ice palace created under the patronage of the Empress Anna may not have been either the first or the largest ever built in Russia, its story is surely the most compelling.

2

Frozen
Construction

Igloos

The first and most famous building of frozen water is, of course, the igloo. The Eskimos of northern Canada use igloos as winter dwellings. By building temporary structures in an extremely cold region, the Eskimos avoid the two main liabilities of ice and snow as construction materials: structural and thermal instability. Structural instability reveals itself in the tendency of snow and ice structures to gradually change their shapes; this phenomenon is called creep. An example of thermal instability is melting.

Aside from these problems, ice—and certain kinds of snow— are surprisingly strong materials. With a tensile strength of about 300 pounds per square inch and a compressive strength of about 1,500 pounds per square inch (at a temperature of 20°F and when rapidly loaded), ice is comparable to concrete. The lower layers of a snowfield, snow milled and packed by modern equipment,

and snow compressed by high winds can also support architectural loads.

The Eskimos pick out strong wind slab snow (compressed by high winds) for their snowhouses. They cut the snow into blocks with a large knife or wood saw and lay the blocks in a spiral course of decreasing diameter. Igloos go up very rapidly, which is useful in case of a sudden blizzard.

After they assemble the dome, the Eskimos fill in all the cracks and light a fire inside—in recent years, a gas cooking stove. When the dome interior begins to soften, they douse the fire and open a vent hole at the igloo zenith. The dripping interior refreezes into a skin of ice. One of the main differences between ice and snow is that ice is impermeable, and the chamber is now sealed off from the outside.

The Eskimos have constructed igloos as large as 20 feet in diameter. They cannot comfortably reach high enough to finish

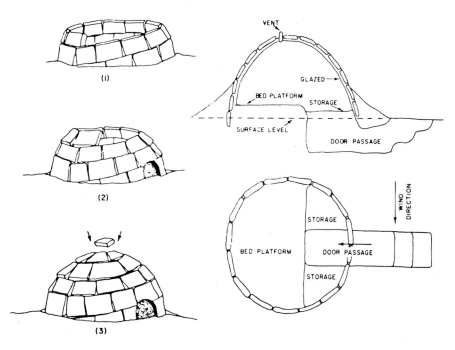

The first and most famous building of frozen water is, of course, the igloo. This diagram shows how to construct one of these domical snowhouses. The Eskimos build with strong snow that has been compressed by high winds.

---

larger domes, and the Arctic offers no suitable materials for scaffolding. But the combination of wind slab snow and a domical form is certainly strong enough to make bigger igloos, if scaffolding were introduced.

Beside using masonry technique to erect the domed chamber, Eskimos carve out part of their house from the snowfield in which it is set. The long entrance tunnel is used for storage as well as to prevent drafts. Outerwear and perishable goods are kept in the cooler tunnel.

Inside their snowhouses, the Eskimos sleep on a raised platform surrounded by the warmest air. They line the chamber with animal skins, which provide a contrast in color and texture to the ubiquitous snow.

One of the major problems of building in the Arctic is snowdrift. The Eskimos minimize it by using a domed structure and by setting the entrance perpendicular to the wind. Another problem of Arctic building is snowfall. Even the sturdiest and most stable of buildings will eventually be buried under new snow, and sooner or later the weight of the snow will destroy it. The nomadic Eskimos simply abandon their igloos and make new ones; modern polar researchers are still trying to figure out how to extend the life of their buildings beyond a few years.

Snow excavation has also been used as a building technique. In 1912, six men from the expedition led by the English explorer Robert Falcon Scott were stranded in Antarctica and lived for six months in an ice cave. They hunted seals to supplement their meager food supply, and they fashioned stoves and lamps from seal blubber and old cans. In 1930, the German Wegener Expedition excavated shelters in the snow near the center of the Greenland Ice Cap, and three members spent the winter there.

Ice Palaces

When the Russians conceived the idea of building temporary festive structures out of ice, they used the same broad categories of technique as the Eskimos: masonry and carving. However, they erected high straight walls instead of small domes, used river ice instead of wind slab snow, relegated carving to the provision of decoration, and introduced water to cement the blocks. When the idea of the ice palace crossed the Atlantic in the nineteenth century, the Canadians and the Americans elaborated on the Russian precedent. The most detailed construction descriptions come from St. Paul, but it is likely that ice architecture techniques were quite uniform throughout North America, at least until the invention of manufactured ice in the twentieth century.

Ice harvesting was a thriving business in the late 1800s. In 1896, the two companies that supplied central St. Paul estimated

Ice harvesters flourished in the late 1800s, and most of their product was sold for refrigeration. In the above picture, however, they apply their skills to gathering ice for the 1887 St. Paul palace.

1. The crew sawed the ice with a special tool, a long piece of steel with a wooden handle.

2. The detached blocks were floated, through a channel, to a landing stage.

3. Horse-drawn pullies hoisted the blocks up the palace walls.

4. Huge tongs gripped the blocks and delivered them where they were needed.

5. Workmen cemented the ice blocks with water.

6. Ice masons trimmed the blocks to fit perfectly into place.

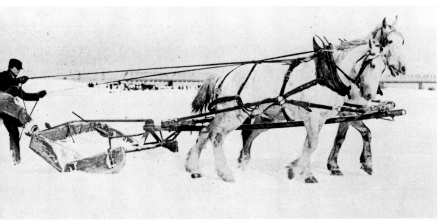

In Montreal in 1910, it was difficult to find ice thick enough to use for construction. Here a worker prepares ice.

Workmen used a sort of plow to mark off huge squares of ice, which were then sawed into suitable sizes for handling.

that they handled between 110,000 and 120,000 tons of ice per year. Most of that ice served to chill food and drink in homes and businesses, not to build ice palaces. The St. Paul brewers generally put up their own ice, and many small dealers sold ice in the suburbs.

Most ice collected for refrigeration was stored close to where it was cut, but a substantial part was brought to town-houses and kept nearer the customers. Layers of sawdust separated the layers of ice. The dealers calculated that only about 10 percent of their annual harvest was lost through melting.

By tradition, cutting commenced after the first of the year. The dealers avoided river ice for home use, reserving it for construction. Lake ice was sometimes preferred for construction as well, because it was clearer and therefore prettier. Ice for the 1887 St. Paul ice palace came from the Mississippi River; Lake Como supplied the 1888 palace.

Certain weather conditions increase ice clarity. In 1896, a sudden intense frost produced exceptionally transparent ice.

The hardened surface of the lakes is twenty inches thick and so clear that one standing on the surface can see distinctly the bottom a few feet away. When taken out in blocks of about four hundred pounds, the ice looks like immense crystals of dazzling clearness. The icemen say that the congealed mass is so clear because of the sharpness and suddenness of the temperature that froze it. A still keen frost following a period of complete calm is necessary to the sort of ice that is being cut this year.[1]

Cool weather facilitated ice cutting as well as ice formation; warm weather made the surface too sloppy. In a warm spell, the crew often switched to working nights.

The crew's first task was "scraping." Using a scraper, pulled by horses, they cleaned the snow and soft ice away. The scraper consisted of:

. . . a straight tongue of strong wood, across the lateral end of which a plank, varying in length from ten to fifteen feet, is fastened on a bevel at an obtuse angle. The lower edge of the plank is sheathed with steel and from the top are two long wooden handles, resembling those of a plow, to which the holder clings while the "scraper" is being drawn over the ice by the horses. The angle at which the plank is set naturally throws the snow to the side in a windrow.[2]

Next the crew employed a "marker," a kind of miniature

Ice blocks were loaded onto horse-drawn sleds, which sped them to the construction site. The blocks shown weighed 1,000 pounds each.

---

ice plow. A strong tongue combined with a long beam to form the marker. A number of steel teeth were set in the beam, and their sharp points dug into the ice as they were drawn over it. A team of horses pulled the marker over a large area of ice, leaving a pattern of parallel lines. Then the team changed its direction and etched a checkerboard in the ice. Since the teeth were adjustable, blocks of various sizes could be laid out. The crew ran the marker repeatedly over the outer lines of the checkerboard, until they succeeded in detaching it from the main body of ice. (A channel had previously been cut, so that open water flowed to the landing stage.) The marker made a high, hissing sound, which contrasted "with the dull, harsh rasp of the 'scraper.'"[3]

One or two workers with pike poles jumped onto the detached mass of ice and pushed it to the landing stage. There they employed another specialized tool, an ice saw:

. . . a long, wide strip of thin, tempered steel, with heavy and not over-sharp teeth. To one end of the saw is attached a round piece of wood resembling an augur handle. This is held by the sawyer, who goes to the center edge of the ice and thrusting the saw into the water begins an up and down motion like an old-fashioned saw mill, and walking backwards follows the line designated by the marker, the teeth of the saw tearing their way through the ice after him.[4]

If very large blocks had been marked out, the saw was used directly on the ice field and individual blocks were pushed to the landing stage. Sometimes a worker rode a block through the channel, for sport, and sometimes he lost his balance and splashed into the chilly water.

At the landing stage, the crew used hooks, poles, and tongs to lift the blocks from the water. The blocks were loaded onto sleds, then rushed to the construction site. Observers naturally delighted in watching ice cutting—now, alas, a vanished art. "These blocks of 400 pounds are really handled with wonderful facility and the amount of ice stowed away in a short space of time is immense. For ice is heavy."[5] Ice weighs approximately 57½ pounds per cubic foot. But crews worked so quickly that less than an hour from the time scraping began, loaded sleds were leaving for the construction site.

Spectators often surrounded the place where an ice palace was being built. Because of the large size of the ice blocks (42 inches by 24 inches by 15 inches for the Montreal palace of 1883), the structures progressed rapidly, growing up before the very eyes of the delighted visitors.

First the workmen unloaded the glassy blocks from the sleds. Then horse-powered pullies lifted the blocks up the ice palace walls. Each piece of ice was secured during its ascent by "heavy ice tongs—whose hard, sharp points securely grip the glistening block as it swings through the air, twisting and turning as though eager to release itself from the iron talons."[6] At the top of the wall, workmen (who had gotten there themselves by climbing scaffolding) took the blocks and trimmed them to fit perfectly in place. They cemented the blocks with water, either sprinkling it over them or pouring it into the seams and crevices. In St. Paul in

1887, it took little more than a minute to lay and cement one block.

At the feet of the palace's round towers, workmen carried out another step. Before the blocks of ice were hoisted, they had to be transformed in shape. A mason would draw the necessary curved outline and carve it out with an axe.

From time to time, a block would escape the grip of the tongs,

. . . crashing down among the blocks below, disfiguring their outlines and unfitting itself for a position in the palace walls. When this occurs, the builders yell, "Look out, there!" while the drivers shout "whoa," and the tongs are quickly lowered, another block clutched, and the work goes on as though nothing had happened.[7]

Much more rarely, a serious accident would occur. In St. Paul in 1888, a workman died after falling from an ice palace turret. Ernst Hoempel fell 65 feet onto the ice shavings inside the tower. A large man, unmarried and German, Hoempel seems to have been an overly exuberant fellow. The *Dispatch* reports that "he had been repeatedly warned to be more careful."[8]

Because of the great size of the blocks, ice palaces went up very rapidly. Such large crowds gathered to watch the construction of this 1895 Ottawa castle that they became a nuisance. The Construction Committee finally reduced their numbers—and raised some money—by charging admission to the site.

3
Castles
in Montreal

Charming, quaint, and cold, Montreal at the turn of the century provided the perfect setting for the first North American ice palace. One-hundred-forty-three years had passed since the building of Empress Anna's villa of ice; Queen Victoria ruled the British Empire; and later in the same year the Brooklyn Bridge would open.

A Montreal writer encouraged visitors to snowshoe with the local people: "Roughness, incivility, or misbehavior of any kind never occurs, and a tramp over the Mountain is as free from any rudeness as a stroll on St. James Street."

Charming, quaint, and cold, Montreal at the turn of the century provided the perfect setting for the first North American ice palace. The city nestles between the St. Lawrence River and the 764-foot-high Mount Royal. During Carnival week, all the Montreal toboggan slides were free to visitors.

Architect A. C. Hutchison designed a simple castle as the centerpiece for a winter carnival. This forerunner palace tested out the qualities and capabilities of ice and led to the construction of larger and more elaborate structures. The experiment amply demonstrated the material's beauty. Clear winter sunlight shone through the castle "in a gorgeous aquamarine . . . the colors of auroral brilliance changed with each step the gazer took."[1] Sunset lent it a deep, mellow glow.

The "commercial capital of Canada" was an elegant, friendly place, vigorously French and English in culture and picturesque to visitors from the south. An American reporter described "the ancient Church of Bonsecour, the oldest Catholic church in Montreal, dark with its memories of the past" and "the quaint old market-place, where habitants in odd-looking costumes sell their meat and vegetables, and fat old French Canadian women barter frozen cream and eggs, a strange preparation of corn boiled in lye, and many other delicacies in name and manufacture incom-

In the 1800s, winter parades consisted of floats on horse-drawn sleds. The participants dressed in costumes; devils often shook their pitchforks at the excited crowd. "The bells merrily jingle. The sleighs swiftly glide over the packed snow on the streets. Silvery laughter floats upon the frosty air; clouds of frozen breath encircle the horses' heads. The long palpitating pageant of horses, sleighs, men, women and waving plumes and ribbons seems to lengthen as it passes." This description from the 1889 St. Paul Dispatch *applies equally well to parades in Montreal.*

prehensible to the stranger." From St. Helen's Island, exactly opposite Montreal, this writer admired the city's beauty. Through the veiling mist rising from the ice-bound St. Lawrence River, he saw Montreal nestled at the base of the 764-foot-high Mount Royal, "dark against the wintry sky." The city's "many church towers and curious old wharves are seen through the mist, shining golden pink in the sunlight."[2]

After praising Montreal's good food and low prices, another American reporter commented on its exoticism:

It is so strange to see the flakes forever falling long after the roads and sidewalks are covered deep with snow, so odd to see the priests in great fur coats, so queer to find sisters of charity in furs, to see babies pushed about in baby sleds, to read that lawyers call themselves "avocats" or "notaires," to run across policemen so bundled up that they look like aldermen, to find that you can tell a stranger because of his high silk hat or stiff Derby, and to meet an endless file of men in coats of bear or beaver, seal or other hides, and to hear that it costs $1000 to get a good garment of the sort. . . . And half the populace has donned the gaudy uniforms of the snowshoers.[3]

Clearly, the city grew very cold in the winter. Its inhabitants, blessed with a passion for cold weather sports, viewed the climate as an asset, to be generously shared. At the 1882 banquet of the Montreal Snowshoe Club, R. D. McGibbon suggested holding a regular winter sports festival, in order to enjoy and show off the glories of Canadian winter. Tobogganers, skaters, and the press eagerly joined the enthusiastic *raquetteurs* (snowshoers) in forming a carnival committee.

The most prominent promoters of the festival were the Marquis of Lorne, Governor General of Canada, and his consort, the Princess Louise. Their encouragement gave the carnival cachet. Social events, such as a grand ball and a costume ball, were mixed in with such sporting activities as snowshoeing, tobogganing, skiing, and curling, a game of Scottish origin in which stones are slid over ice toward a target.

Ideal weather helped to make the 1883 Winter Carnival a resounding success. Tourists packed the trains coming into Montreal. After all the hotels filled up, owners of private houses charged high prices for their hospitality. An estimated 15,000 foreign visitors flocked to the city, including the Vanderbilts from New York. Papers in other cities featured the carnival; it was covered on the front page of *The New York Times*.

McGibbon's inauguration of the ice palace was one of the highlights of the *fête*. "All the avenues of approach to the spot were almost inextricably crowded with spectators, on foot, on horse, and in vehicle. There must have been from twenty-five to thirty thousand persons present." [4]

The ice palace was designed by A. C. Hutchison, senior partner in the Montreal firm of Hutchison & Steele. At the age of nineteen, Hutchison had supervised the cut-stone work of Christ Church Cathedral. Later, in Ottawa, he took charge of the cut-stone work on a part of the Parliament Buildings. By 1883, he had been practicing architecture for about twenty-one years. Among his buildings still standing are the Redpath Museum at McGill University and Erskine and American Church on Sherbrooke Street. After the tremendous success of Montreal's first ice palace, A. C. Hutchison went on to design the palaces of 1884, 1885, and 1887. He was the architect of the 1886 castle in St. Paul, and probably of Montreal's 1889 castle as well.

A. C. Hutchison came from a construction-oriented family. His father, a builder, erected the Bank of Montreal, the Bank of British North America, St. Andrew's Church, and Mount St. Mary Convent. His brother, J. H. Hutchison, served as contractor on the 1883 ice palace.

J. H. Hutchison supervised a crew of fifty men. At the frozen St. Lawrence River they cut blocks of ice, which measured 42 inches by 24 inches by 15 inches and weighed 500 pounds each. The castle, like all other nineteenth-century ice

The Indians invented the toboggan, a flat-bottomed sled, as a means of transporting game and other goods through the Québec forests. Early toboggans often were pulled by teams of dogs. Their lightness and broad lower surface enabled them to run over deep snow without sinking.

The first North American ice palace was built in Montreal in 1883, to serve as the centerpiece for a carnival of winter sports. Rising from a square floor plan, it was one of the few roofed ice palaces. The builders arranged beams and green boughs into peaked roofs, and covered them with water, which froze into icicles. FACING, AND ABOVE, LEFT

Architect A. C. Hutchison designed the Montreal ice palaces of 1883, 1884, 1885, 1887, and 1889, as well as the St. Paul ice palace of 1886. As a young man, he took charge of part of the cut-stone work on the Canadian Parliament buildings. ABOVE, RIGHT

castles in Montreal, was assembled in the lower half of Dominion Square, in the area now known as Place du Canada.

The palace would have fit neatly within a 90-foot cube. Its plan was approximately square; its outer walls were about 90 feet long and 20 feet high. The steeple topping the main tower, which stood in the building's center, reached 90 feet in height. Fifty-foot-tall towers rose at each of the castle's four corners. All the towers rose from square bases.

This was one of the few roofed ice palaces. The construction crew built peaked structures of beams and green boughs on top of the ice block walls. Then they poured water over the roofs, and the water froze into sheets of icicles.

Sixteen electric lights illuminated the castle at night. "They were enough to make it gleam and glint in the darkness of a winter's night, like a fantasy out of the Arabian nights."[5]

In the 1880s, electric light itself was still a novelty. All the newspapers remarked on the lighting, which became a regular feature of subsequent palaces.

1884

In the United States, Grover Cleveland took office as president. In Montreal, a carnival took place that was even grander than that of 1883. The Governor General of Canada and his wife, the Marquess and Marchioness of Lansdowne, attended as guests of honor. This being Lord Lansdowne's first visit to Montreal, he was greeted by a Canadian invention, a "Living Arch." The first living arch had welcomed the Marquis of Lorne to Montreal in 1878, and the custom of erecting these structures to honor visiting dignitaries continues to the present day.

Like ice palaces, living arches are structures built purely for admiration and amusement. A wooden scaffold, in the form of a full-scale triumphal arch, supports a display. The 1884 arch symbolized winter sports and featured snowshoes, toboggans, and evergreen branches. Hundreds of snowshoers, dressed in

On the covers of carnival programs and special carnival editions of newspapers, artists illustrated the delights of winter. On the left, a program cover depicts the icy season as a white-bearded king. On the right, a couple of snowshoers take a stroll in typical snowshoeing attire.

colorful traditional costumes, climbed the framework and took their assigned places to form a *tableau vivant*. "A living group forms one of the two family crests borne by Lord Lansdowne, a

bee hive. . . . The word 'Welcome' is spelled out with snowshoes of various sizes."[6]

The traditional snowshoe costume, mentioned above, generally consists of a blanket suit, a sash, a tuque, and, of course, snowshoes. *Tuque* is the French Canadian name for a warm knitted stocking cap. The colors of a snowshoer's ensemble identify the club of which he is a member. *The New York Times* describes the outfits of the Montreal clubs: "There is the white coat, purple

Each year, the studio of famous photographer William Notman prepared an official composite picture of the carnival. This composite centers on the 1884 ice palace.

tuque, and knickerbockers of the St. George's Club, with the cross of St. George, the blue suit of Le Trappeur, the green of the Emerald, the red tuque and legging of the Montreal, and the stripes of the Argyles, to say nothing of a host of lesser clubs."[7]

The 1884 Carnival had an official picture, a composite photograph showing the main events of the festival, prepared by the studio of Wm. Notman & Son, "with the co-operation of the various sporting clubs of Montreal."[8] Notman, one of the great nineteenth-century photographers, took many of the photographs that record different ice palaces and carnivals and that served as bases for drawings and paintings of these phenomena.

The first day of the carnival, February 4, 1884, saw the inauguration of the ice palace. Firework displays were held there every evening. Carnival sporting competitions included a hockey tournament, a curling bonspiel (tournament), trotting races at Driving Park, lacrosse on skates, a 15-mile race at Victoria

Skating Rink, and a snowshoe steeplechase over Mount Royal.

Visitors were encouraged to join the Montrealers in skating, snowshoeing, and tobogganing. A "Grand Sleighing Parade" was held. The most elegant and largest skating rink, the Victoria, issued special tickets for Carnival week, at three dollars for gentlemen and two dollars for ladies. Dawson's guide to the *Montreal Winter Carnival* mentions that, in addition to several rinks, "on the river are many places swept and kept in order where a skate may be had for five or ten cents." Dawson urges tourists to snowshoe with the natives:

Strangers are always welcome and may depend upon kindly and hospitable treatment, if they join any of these tramping excursions. Roughness, incivility, or misbehaviour of any kind never occurs, and a tramp over the Mountain is as free from any rudeness as a stroll on St. James Street. Sometimes the exuberant spirits of the young men break out into song, and the frosty air rings to the chorus of 'Alouette,' or some other local melody; but the only exhilarants are the bright moonshine on the glittering snow, the rapid movement, and the keen frosty air.[9]

All the tobogganing slides were free to visitors during Carnival week. Dawson's *Montreal Winter Carnival* promises that any friendly visitor who perfects the sport, by inventing a way of sliding up, will be commemorated by a statue in ice.

The social events of the carnival included a fancy dress (costume) ball at the Crystal Skating Rink, two grand fancy dress balls at the Victoria Rink, and a grand ball at the Windsor Hotel. A miniature ice temple, grotto, and fountains rose from the center of the Victoria Rink. On Thursday and Friday evenings, the Caughnawaga Indians gave concerts in the Iroquois language. "There will be war dances, and tableaux illustrating scalping, election of chiefs, and other pleasing evocations of the heroic days of Montreal."[10]

Wednesday night all the snowshoe clubs of the area took part in a grand torchlight procession, climaxing in the "storming of the ice palace." In this ritual, some snowshoe clubs attacked the palace with fireworks, such as rockets, Roman candles, and

This picture of the 1884 Montreal ice palace comes from the Notman Studio. The palace stretched 160 by 64 feet; its tower stood 80 feet tall.

bombs, while other clubs defended it with the same weapons. That evening, "'there was hardly a spot on Dominion Square that had not some occupant.' Several wooden stands had been put up to give visitors a clear view. The palatial Windsor Hotel 'was a blaze of lights from bottom to top, and every window was filled with ladies and gentlemen.'"[11]

The ice palace of 1884 attained greater dimensions than that of 1883. It consisted of 10,000 to 15,000 blocks of ice and cost about $3,200 Canadian. The building stretched 160 feet in length; its width varied from 64 feet at the center to 48 feet at the ends.

Its glory, the tower, reached 80 feet. It was slightly shorter than the previous year's tower, but in this case the peak was achieved entirely with blocks of ice, rather than with beams and green boughs. Three discrete sections comprised the tower. The base was 20 feet square and 40 feet high; its walls were 6 feet 9 inches thick at the bottom. The middle section, about 16 feet square in plan and 16 feet high, was set diagonally on the lowest

section. The topmost stage was octagonal in plan, 20 feet high, and surmounted with battlements.

The eastern end of the palace terminated in an apse; the sun set over a square end. Four towers, each 13 feet square, defended the corners of the building. Porches, 14 feet by 18 feet, lay at the front and back; there were four entrances. The curtain walls joining the main building with the flanks were 22 feet high; the part of the main building adjoining the central tower rose to a height of 28 feet.[12]

1885

The 1885 Carnival ran from January 26 to January 31. Activities paralleled those of the year before, and generally remained the same throughout the nineteenth century. Tobogganing was always a favorite; the 1885 *Montreal Witness* Carnival Number informs us that the Lansdowne slide, standing on a natural declivity north of Mount Royal, ran a total distance of some 2,500 feet. On the first night of carnival, the Montreal toboggan slide was illuminated with colored Chinese transparencies, flaring torches, and a huge bonfire.

Three unique features of the 1885 Carnival were the lion, the condora, and the volcano. The mammoth ice lion was unveiled on the evening of January 26, in a blaze of electric light and fireworks. The beast measured 16 feet in length. It rested in the Place d'Armes, on a pedestal some 20 feet high, with a base diameter of 21 feet. The pedestal, cruciform in plan, receded in steps as it rose, the top being 6 feet broad. Between each of the angles lay a row of rounded ice steps, over which water poured. The interior of the structure was lit by electric and colored light at night.

The 1884 Montreal ice palace was the focus of an extremely successful carnival. Canadian Governor General Lord Lansdowne and his wife made their first visit to Montreal to be the guests of honor.

Place d'Armes-square is small, but it is surrounded by some remarkably fine buildings, and no fitter place could have been chosen to show to advantage the colossal proportions of the ice lion. . . . The brilliant light reflected from the glittering back and the proud, uplifted head of the huge lion shone full upon the grand face and towering steeples of the parish church, the great church of Notre Dame just across the street, and even brought to view the cowering forms of the saints in the niches above the heavy doors, and making a picture which those who saw it will never forget.[13]

The ''Egyptian condora,'' ''tower of Babel,'' or ''ice cairn'' almost rivaled the palace in size. It rose 75 feet high, from a circular base 75 feet in diameter. Twelve thousand blocks of ice were used in its construction.

This conical marvel was designed by Théodose Daoust, who later designed the ice palaces of 1909 and 1910. Set on the Champ de Mars, it consisted of seven stories, circled by eight small towers. A colossal figure, dressed in the costume of ''Le Trappeur'' Snowshoe Club, stood on the pinnacle and held in its

The Montreal Carnival Committee wanted to make each ice castle bigger and more spectacular than the one before. The 1885 palace was elliptical in plan, with a long axis of 160 feet. Its tower stood 100 feet tall. FACING

This winter troika heralded the arrival of the 1885 Carnival. In the background, tobogganers, sleigh riders, and dancers frolic by moonlight. BELOW, LEFT *The* Montreal Witness *sold this special 1885 carnival edition for ten cents.* BELOW, RIGHT

hand a torch, lit at night by electricity. "The whole building is also illuminated at dark by the electric light; by this, a very pretty effect is produced, owing to the extreme beauty of the soft tint of the ice cut from the bosom of the noble River St. Lawrence."[14]

The volcano, built of snow and ice, erupted in displays of fireworks. It was located on St. Helen's Island, a "gem of sylvan beauty." For the carnival, the Montrealers connected the island to the city by constructing a grand boulevard across the river. St. Helen's also featured a "hunters' camp." Amid the tall bare trees stood a small square house of cedar logs, of the kind inhabited by the North American pioneers.[15]

The Carnival Committees each year intended to make their ice castle larger and grander than its predecessors. The 1885 scheme, again conceived by A. C. Hutchison, was erected with 12,000 blocks of ice, at a cost of about $5,000. The plan was elliptical, the major axis stretching 160 feet, the minor axis 120 feet. At each end of the major axis stood an oblong tower, 38 feet high, pierced by an entrance to the interior. At each end of the minor axis were placed two round towers, which rose to heights of 44 feet; between the towers were arched entrances.

The main tower reached 100 feet. Double towers flanked it on one side, single towers on the other. The double towers rose to heights of 40 and 50 feet respectively, the single towers rose to 70 feet.

The New York Times describes the palace's beauty:

It is wonderfully beautiful in the daylight, but it is not until evening that one sees to perfection the enchanted castle of gleaming sea-green united ice, when with the moon shining in the heavens above with that clear brilliancy seen only in extremely cold countries, and with the electric illuminations glittering through its towers and turrets, it seems much more like the marvelous imaginings of some opium sated dream than a real tangible thing. . . .[16]

Since the building's design was drawn up before Christmas, several publishers used it for cards, which were eagerly purchased by the Montrealers.

At least 100,000 people gathered for the storming of the ice palace on January 28. The mock battle delighted the spectators.

Around the fairy-like structure is the girdle of the white-blanketed attacking force drawn up in military array and awaiting the signal for the assault. A faint red glow colors the sparkling white walls, and a fiery rocket shoots with a loud report into the air. It is the signal for the attack. A volley of fire blazes forth from the front rank of the besieging force, a ready return belches forth from each loophole, bastion, and turret of the palace, and the mimic battle rages in all its apparent fury until the whole of the vast space surrounding the palace is fairly alive with every conceivable kind of fiery colored missile.[17]

1886

A smallpox epidemic struck Montreal in the summer of 1885, killing more than 2,000 people in a few weeks. Although the city's hotels and sporting clubs yearned to hold the usual winter carnival, they were stopped by American authorities, who kept the province of Quebec in quarantine. (From discussions reported by *The New York Times*, it seems that even if the 1886 Montreal Carnival *had* taken place, it probably would have lacked an ice palace, since the St. Lawrence ice did not thicken until unusually late that winter.) The citizens of St. Paul, Minnesota, stepped into the gap, organized their first carnival, and hired A. C. Hutchison to design the ice palace.

1887

By 1887 Montreal had recovered from the epidemic, and its reinstated winter carnival was as well attended as ever. The Wagner Sleeping Car Company reported that every available sleeping car in the New York area was needed to transport New Yorkers to the

---

"The storming of the ice palace" was an exciting mock battle and fireworks show. This lithograph of the 1885 ice palace also shows, in the upper-right-hand corner, the ice condora, a frozen "tower of Babel" 75 feet tall.

After a smallpox epidemic in 1886, Montreal resumed holding winter carnivals in 1887. The 1887 ice palace was described as "a house of alabaster by day and a giant lantern of crystal by night."   FACING

The 1887 ice palace, one of the few asymmetrical ones, housed a handsome rink for skating and hockey. It had four towers, the tallest of which reached 102 feet.   TOP, RIGHT

The plan of the 1887 ice maze copied, in a smaller form, the famous maze at Hampton Court in England. A hot drink rewarded the explorer who solved the puzzle.   BOTTOM, RIGHT

The Montreal Tandem Club sponsored a grand sleigh drive during each carnival. Clubs and individuals rode in their most splendid rigs. The 1889 St. Paul Dispatch *Carnival Edition provides an apt commentary: "Stately-stepping steeds; champing their bits; tossing their proud heads; throwing flecks of frozen foam above them; drawing superb sleighs of every graceful shape, filled with pretty women enveloped in furs and wearing the colors of the club they favor."*   BELOW

Like ice palaces, living arches are structures built to delight. This 60-foot-high living arch, built in 1887, celebrated the fiftieth year of Queen Victoria's reign. A wooden scaffold supported a display of evergreens, toboggans, snowshoes, and snowshoers. TOP, LEFT

Snowshoers cheered and sang as the Governor General's procession passed beneath this living arch in 1889. CENTER

Fancy dress skating balls were an important part of every Montreal carnival. The Victoria Rink and the Crystal Rink competed for elegant guests. RIGHT

Dawson's Winter Carnival *explains: ''A true French-Canadian is fond of swift locomotion, and will never walk if anything with four legs can be got to drag him.''* FACING

carnival. For thirty-five dollars a day, a Wagner car complete with services of cook, porter, and conductor could be rented by a visitor and used as his Montreal hotel.

Americans traveled to Montreal by train in large parties:

Ordinary travelers who went to the Grand Central Station for the Chicago express last evening might well have imagined themselves dropped suddenly into a camp of Esquimaux. Seated on the benches and walking about the station were figures, presumably female, wrapped to the ears in furs, and men loaded down with extra overcoats, blankets, ulsters, and other paraphernalia suited to a climate which knows no thaw from Fall until Spring. The departure of the Chicago train was the signal for a general massing of effects among those who waited, and when the train door again opened everybody proceeded to stow himself and herself, with his or her bundles, into the special cars bound for Montreal. There were seven sleeping cars, and not one of them had a spare berth.[18]

The foreign ladies made a special contribution to the Montreal Carnival: " . . . if stories are to be believed there will be no blanket suits more stylish on the streets of the icy city during the week than those of New York design."[19]

Although well-attended, the carnival faltered in one respect. Sporting men complained that all the money was devoted to display and practically none to sport. In addition, the weather, exceedingly variable and generally rainy, totally ruined this already weakened segment of activity.

The display, on the other hand, scintillated. A particularly memorable living arch, "The Queen's Jubilee Arch," celebrated the fiftieth year of Queen Victoria's reign. Constructed at the corner of McGill and St. James streets, it rose to a height of 60 feet.

A new structure, an ice maze, occupied the whole Place d'Armes Square. The plan copied, in a smaller form, the celebrated maze at Hampton Court in England. From the outside, the ice labyrinth resembled a medieval tower, protected by a circular outwork, reinforced by four bastions and breeched by four portals. The diameter of the outer wall was 72 feet, the height of the central tower 40 feet. Low walls of ice divided the area within the outer walls into a series of circular walks.[20] The explorer who reached the central tower was rewarded with "something hot."[21]

Writer Julian Ralph described the 1887 palace as "a house of alabaster by day and a giant lantern of crystal by night."[22] About 25,000 blocks of ice went into its construction, and the outer walls stretched 144 feet by 110 feet. It housed a handsome rink for skating and hockey contests.

The castle differed from former ones in that the principal tower was located at the northwestern corner of the building rather than in its center. This tower rose to a height of 102 feet. Each of the other three corners of the building boasted its own distinct tower. These towers attained heights of 80, 50, and 32 feet.

For the storming of the ice palace, a Gatling gun was intro-

duced into the main tower. When the Snowshoers' Phalanx attacked, the gun discharged volleys of colored fire. Every Montreal athletic club, as well as twenty-three from the United States and other Canadian cities, participated in the mock battle. The Boston Snowshoe Club, the Columbia Snowshoe Club of St. Paul, and the Mountain Toboggan Club of New York were among those represented.

Unfortunately, the storming proved more explosive than anyone expected.

A large supply of fireworks had been placed in readiness in each of the towers, but no precautions were taken to cover them up from sparks, and consequently one lot after another took fire and rockets and roman candles were sent whizzing among the garrisons. The men in the towers were enveloped in smoke and flame and had to slide down the ladder to get out of the way. Then the reserve ammunitions in the centre of the castle took fire and caused an explosion that shook the walls. The garrisons were running hither and thither to get out of the way of the rockets, which were flying in all directions. . . . The most serious accident was the explosion of a bomb of half-inch cast iron. . . . One part of the bomb struck the rear and another the side wall, knocking large holes in the ice. A third piece struck the northwest tower, and threw down a mass of ice, which crashed through a coffee stand where a number of people were standing. . . .[23]

The explosions broke the arm of the gentleman in charge of the bombs, burned almost every man in the garrison, and killed one lady who was watching the spectacle. At the next firework display, the bombs were discharged from the brow of the mountain, and no further tragedies occurred.

1889

In the year the Eiffel Tower opened in Paris, the Montreal Winter Carnival ran into a series of problems. During construction of the

---

This lithograph depicts the ice palace of 1889 as it was intended to be. Beset by problems, it never attained its full grandeur.

ice palace, a severe thaw set in and the west wall melted away. Although a cold snap enabled the workers to rebuild the wall, the palace no longer presented a uniform appearance. The blocks of ice forming the walls had lost their square edges, and cracks of two inches or more appeared between the layers. A proposal that the fire brigade spray the structure until it became a mass of gleaming icicles was never acted upon.

A blizzard that began as the visitors were arriving interfered disastrously with the program and rendered outdoor activity extremely uncomfortable. By February 6, many of the tourists decided to board the trains for home. They feared the storm would keep them snowbound if they did not leave at once.

Another factor may also have hastened the visitors' departure. Americans attending the early carnivals had enjoyed Montreal's relatively low prices. For example, one writer praises the sleighs, which served as taxis, driven by "carters"—

. . . small, dark-skinned Frenchmen in caps and great coats of fur. . . . You notice that the horses are also small and swarthy and wiry like the drivers, and you suspect that they must be French also. You are charged carnival prices for riding in one of these multitudinous sleighs, but Montreal carters' fees are so low that even with the carnival inflation they remain moderate; and then you are so comfortable in one, wrapped up in a heavy skin and bolting along at such a lively gait, that you are altogether sorry you did not have a longer journey to make.[24]

By 1889, however, at least one source felt that the Montreal carnival was no longer a bargain. *The Burlington Free Press and Times* reports:

It is not unlikely that the exorbitant and greedy action of the hotel, restaurant and storekeepers and the cabmen, the latter class seemingly trying to steal the unenviable fame of their Niagara Falls brethren, had something to do with the disgusted look on the faces of the American visitors as they took their trains for home. The people of Montreal are not slow in admitting that their carnivals could not be a success were it not for the visitors from the United States and yet they all persist in trying to kill the hen that lays the golden egg. They will succeed one of

During construction of the 1889 ice castle, a warm spell melted the west wall away. The wall was later rebuilt, but cracks and drips marred the palace's original crisp facade.

these days, after which the Montreal winter carnivals will be known only in history.''[25]

The journalist who wrote this account was probably not entirely objective, since his own city had sponsored a rival but less successful carnival.

One pleasing feature of the 1889 Montreal Carnival was the introduction of chimes into the ice tower. The clear-sounding, tubular bells were played at intervals and could be heard for three miles. When the carnival was over, these chimes were acquired by St. Matthias Anglican Church, and for years they sounded over the fields of what is now Westmount.

Despite the defects mentioned, the ice palace made a stirring spectacle. The photographs show that no flaws were apparent from a distance. According to *The Burlington Free Press and Times*, ''the castle presented a magnificent sight when lit up at night with hundreds of electric lights, and a sight of it under these conditions would, to many, be of itself worth the trip to Montreal.''[26]

This last grand ice palace in Dominion Square was fashioned from 25,000 blocks of ice. It measured 164 feet in length, 155 feet in width; the central tower rose 118 feet.

1909

Montreal's great ice-palace-building era ended with the problems of 1889. The idea was not revived until 1909, the year that Admiral Peary reached the North Pole. Two factors short-circuited the new ice palace's chance of success: the sponsors' desire to surpass all previous castles and the fading of the construction experience and techniques that the city had not used for twenty years. In the Middle Ages, years of competition to produce the biggest Gothic cathedral resulted in Beauvais—with its crumbling apse. Years of competition to produce the biggest ice palace resulted in the misfortunes of 1909.

Carnival activities flowed smoothly in 1909. More than 100,000 people turned out for the first storming of the ice palace on February 11. A series of elegant fancy dress balls were reminiscent of the historic masquerade on Shrove Tuesday, March 1, 1870, at which Prince Arthur (later the Duke of Connaught) had been a guest. Complaints were relatively minor: it was felt that additional snow to cover the ice would have made snowshoeing more enjoyable, and that some cabbies had grown extortionist, charging rates of six, eight, or even ten dollars for a two- to three-hour drive.

Théodose Daoust had developed a splendid plan for the ice palace:

It will eclipse everything ever seen in this line. It will be encircled by an ice wall which will stretch from end to end a distance of over 200 feet. . . . A majestic feature will be the King Edward Tower, which will be 190 feet high by 40 feet square. The Prince of Wales Tower, destined to be 95 feet high, with a diameter of 20 feet, and the Queen Alexandra Tower, 85 feet high by 16 feet square, [will stand beside it.] Two arches, approximately 60 feet high, will connect the three towers, and a small tower adjoining the King Edward will furnish a stairway by which the other towers can be reached.[27]

The castle was to employ 250,000 cubic feet of ice and cost

The most successful carnival balls reminded people of this famous skating masquerade in 1870, at which Prince Arthur was an honored guest. At the far left, in a fur hat, the prince stands, slightly larger than life. This group picture is a photographic composite, assembled from many individual portraits, photographed, and painted.

Montreal Carnival of Winter Sport — Ice Palace and Fort.

Montreal's great ice palace building era ended with the problems of 1889. A revival in 1909 and 1910 was less than entirely successful. Théodose Daoust developed a splendid plan for the 1909 palace—The King Edward Tower was supposed to stand 190 feet high—but the castle as built was much less lofty than planned and had a "sawed-off" appearance. ABOVE, LEFT AND RIGHT

Théodose Daoust designed this lovely ice palace for the 1910 Carnival. Churlish weather interfered with its construction. FACING

$7,000; the tower walls were to be 4 feet thick. With a crew of 130 men, the Charles Thackery Company worked at constructing the palace, but unseasonably mild weather interfered with their activity.

Built on Fletcher's Field, the ice palace disappointed even the sympathetic Canadian press: "The building is not quite so picturesque as had been intended, owing to the fact that the contractor was so pressed for time [due to the warm spell] that the Committee judged it was wise to stop work before the principal tower was carried up to the height originally planned. This gives a somewhat "sawed-off" appearance to the top of the structure."[28]

Although the ice palace fell short of expectations, its first storming was spectacular. The new location, on the eastern slope of Mount Royal, had room for about ten times as many people as Dominion Square had held. The flight of two hot air balloons opened the mock battle. The palace's 3,000 electric lights interacted with a rousing show of fireworks. When the showshoers rushed upon the castle, it responded with:

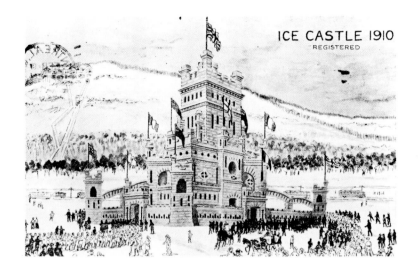

ICE CASTLE 1910
REGISTERED

. . . fan-shaped volleys of stars, columns of stars, clouds of stars, until the air was literally filled with a sea of darting glittering points. Then came fountains and rivers of golden fire with spangles and sparks like molten iron . . . Amid every variety of noise from the sharp ping of rifles to the deafening explosion of mines, bombs and mortar-shells, amid light ranging from a dim candle glow to an intensity that made the whole of Fletcher's Fields brilliant. . . . The blare of trumpets, the ruddy glare of thousands of torches, the quaint snowshoe costumes of blanket suit, tuque and sash, the expectation and excitement of the vast multitude, all combined to make a composite impression not seen in Montreal since the last great carnival of February 7, 1889. . . .[29]

On February 14, 1909, a snowstorm whipped through the city and the temperature hovered near zero. The Carnival Committee arranged for a band and hot beverages to lure visitors into the ice palace. The blizzard lasted for three days.

On the last day of the carnival, February 20, a downpour marred the second storming of the ice palace. Only about 250 snowshoers (as opposed to a couple of thousand at the first storming) participated in the attack. At the end of the show, as the crowd was moving away, a noise like thunder rumbled and half the Alexandra tower collapsed!

H. F. Tibbs was in the tower at the time, packing up his company's exhibit. He saw the electric lights go out and heard a huge roar as the structure crumbled around him. "Mr. Tibbs said he thought his end had come, but as soon as he realized that he was still alive he quickly groped his way out."[30] Safely outside, he paid two bystanders five dollars each to rescue his show cases.

1910

The following year, a typhoid epidemic almost caused the cancellation of the carnival, but in the end it materialized. The Carnival Committee again hired Théodose Daoust as architect, and he came up with an excellent plan. If the palace had been built according to his design, it would have matched the beauty of any of its rivals.

J. B. Corriveau & Brunet secured the building contract. Five derricks were used in erecting the palace. The firm of Napoleon Archambault cut the ice from Back River. The Hamilton & National Fireworks Co. of Boston promised to provide "the greatest pyrotechnical display ever witnessed on this continent."[31]

As in the previous year, the finished building failed to fulfill the original conception. A thaw set in about January 18 that caused construction to be halted. Four about ten days the building melted, but finally the frost returned and a crew of seventy men rushed to repair and complete it.

They were only partially successful. They never built the grand arches that were to have connected the extreme corner towers to the central tower. The middle walls, designed to reach 50 feet, only attained about half that height. The central tower, planned to scale 100 feet, stood only about 65 feet tall.

Arc lamps illuminated the 1910 ice palace. Six were set up in the main tower, one in each of the annex towers, and one in each of the corner towers. Ten more were distributed about the courtyard. A picturesque storming took place on February 1, but the fireworks display, on February 3, was "not so extensive as in former years."[32]

4

Cathedrals
in St. Paul

1886

Eighteen-eighty-six "was the year that the tuxedo was introduced in Tuxedo Park, New York. The American Federation of Labor was founded in Ohio. Geronimo, the famous Apache warrior, was captured. The Statue of Liberty was unveiled, and the malted milk and electric street railway came into existence."[1] That same year, a smallpox outbreak ravaged Montreal and forced the cancellation of its winter carnival. The Canadian city's misfortune provided St. Paul, Minnesota, with an opportunity.

St. Paul, overlooking the Mississippi River, was America's fastest-growing city in 1886. Its population had swelled from

When a smallpox epidemic canceled Montreal's winter carnival in 1886, St. Paul stepped into the gap. The St. Paul carnival featured all kinds of sporting activities. Six toboggan slides were built on Cedar Street, and the Finch Slide extended over 1,500 feet.

39,000 in 1880 to 120,000 six years later. Minnesota's capital city had become America's third largest rail center, with sixteen main lines terminating in its front yard. The previous year, 1885, had been a time of business depression and low prices for the country as a whole, but in St. Paul the natural processes of local development had called "for the grading of nearly 20 miles of streets, the placing of 11 miles of sewers, and the laying of 23½ miles of water mains."[2]

St. Paul's business leaders decided to demonstrate their success and celebrate "the magnificent climate of Minnesota."[3] They had been outraged earlier by a New York newspaper correspondent who had described their beloved city as "another Siberia, unfit for human habitation in winter."[4] They met in the glamorous new Ryan Hotel and established the St. Paul Winter Carnival Association. Incorporated for a thirty-year period, the Association planned to sponsor a festival and an ice palace each

"Eight miles of streets will be radiant with light, clusters of colored gas globes appearing every fifty feet, while at the junctions of the streets will be discovered graceful gas arches, or massive arches of evergreens, from among whose foliage gleam forth bright sparks of fire." LEFT

The St. Paul Dispatch *produced this colorful cover for a special edition about the 1888 Carnival. Many St. Paul publications imported New York artists to paint memorable carnival illustrations.* RIGHT

year. One of its first acts, following the suggestion of local architect C. E. Joy, was to bring in A. C. and J. H. Hutchison from Montreal to design and build the palace.

At that time, Third Street, now called Kellogg Boulevard, dominated St. Paul. The city hall and court house were located at Fourth and Cedar streets. Central Park, located near what is now the Minnesota Capitol, served as a recreational focus.

The Carnival Association chose Central Park as the site for

Sportsmen could choose among showshoeing, tobogganing, skating, curling, polo, and lacrosse. And each year the Carnival Association built an ice palace. (St. Paul, 1886) ABOVE

The frozen Mississippi River became a highway for horse-drawn sleighs. TOP, RIGHT

To the people of St. Paul, carnival has always meant fantastic parades. This horse-drawn sled served as a float in 1886. BOTTOM, RIGHT

the ice palace. They raised a fence around the park grounds, and set admission at twenty-five cents for adults and ten cents for children. Within the grounds were an encampment of seventy-five Sioux Indians, which delighted the visitors, an exhibition hall, a baseball diamond, and rinks for curling, skating, polo, and lacrosse. Six toboggan slides were built on Cedar Street, with the long and lofty Finch Slide extending for a distance of more than

St. Paul business leaders imported Montreal architect A. C. Hutchison to design St. Paul's first ice palace. Well-known St. Paul photographer Ingersoll took this picture of the 1886 castle.

1,500 feet. Carnival activities included skiing, snowshoeing, a blanket tossing contest, and pushball, a game played with giant balls.

"The Crystal Carnival" poetically described the carnival park: "The stalwart sons of Scotia impel the polished stones o'er glassy ice, and dusky denizens of the dark North woods gambol with their wolfish dogs before their skin tepees; muscular youths in bright apparel skillfully pilot laughing maidens down the steep toboggan slide, rivaling the wind in boisterous speed."[5]

The region around the city abounded in natural beauties. Hills and vales alternated with glassy lakes and the Mississippi and Minnesota rivers. Old Fort Snelling, recommended to sightseers, stood on the point of a lofty bluff, located between the rivers and encircled by meadows. Adventurous visitors could make their own toboggan slides and snowshoe trails in the picturesque countryside.

The carnival featured social activities as well. "The Crystal Carnival" stated that visitors to St. Paul "will find society, cultured and refined, and a hearty hospitality which will delight them. Amusements of the best class will be furnished at the Grand Opera House and the other theaters and museums, while fancy dress, masquerade, and other elegant balls will be frequent during the carnival at the various halls."[6] Good weather helped to make the 1886 carnival such a success that it was extended to run for all of February.

St. Paulites have fabricated various "ancient legends" to account for their ice palaces and the dazzling displays of fireworks around them. The earliest recorded legend appeared in "The Crystal Carnival" in 1886. In this version, King Borealis of the North and his queen leave their home in "the icy caverns of the crystallized region beyond the ken of man" and come to live in the St. Paul ice palace. However, the Fire King, also known as Shawondasee, King of the Summer, grows jealous of the honor shown to Borealis. Shawondasee attacks the castle with fireworks. "Instantly the dense ranks of the besieging army break into flame—scarlet, and purple, and blue, and yellow." The defenders rise to the occasion and repel the assault. "From every battlement and peak and tower a sudden sheet of fire goes up; rockets and mortars and bombshells and fountains of flame."[7]

"For one brief week nothing occurs to disturb the harmony of the Ice King's reign, and the festivities increase in elegance and novelty."[8] Next, however, an army of mortals besieges the palace, and to this final storming Borealis succumbs. One concession is made to the brave old Ice King: "that each year for thirty years there should be a palace of ice builded in the capital city for his winter festivities."[9]

The carnival whirl revolved around the ice palace. The Carnival Association sold stock (at ten dollars a share) to raise the $5,210 it cost. J. H. Hutchison combined with Brodie, a local contractor, and employed 200 men for the three-week building period.

The unit of construction was the ice block, measuring 22 inches by 32 inches by 18 inches. Estimates of the number of blocks used range from 20,000 to over 30,000. At the ice mines of the Mississippi River and Lake Como, the frozen blocks were marked, measured, and hand-cut with giant saws. About twenty ice-hauling crews, using fast horses and oversize sleds, rushed

Each of the first three St. Paul ice palaces took the form of a dominant tower, defended by outworks. The central tower of the 1886 castle stood 106 feet tall.

51

the blocks to the building site. In addition, outlying towns, some as far distant as the Dakotas, donated chunks of ice.

Each of the three great St. Paul ice palaces (1886, 1887, and 1888) took the form of a dominant tower, defended by outworks. A. C. Hutchison's 1886 effort measured 180 feet by 154 feet by 106 feet in height. In the center rose a massive square tower, with smaller round towers at each corner. Battlements capped all the towers and walls of the building; embrasures penetrated it rhythmically. The main tower was defended by an outwork 32 feet high. The outer walls measured 20 inches thick; those of the central tower, 40 inches. Four grand arched entrances led into the palace.

An observer reports:

The magnificent pile of glittering ice, when seen beneath the bright rays of the winter sun, or at night when illuminated by the white electric lights and fires of varied hues, presents an effect which is simply impossible to describe. . . . Impressive as is the effect of the palace as viewed from the outside, the full beauty of it is not experienced until its gleaming interior is seen. It is divided into great apartments, spacious halls, vast corridors and wide chambers, all with walls transparent and glistening.[10]

Each entrance led into a 40-foot high hallway, flanked by two anterooms (each 6 feet by 5 feet in plan). Beyond each hall lay an apartment, about 15 feet square. Opening from it to either the right or left, through carved archways, was a room 28 feet square and 40 feet high. Directly beyond, at the heart of the palace, was the grand tower room, 26 feet square. The palace was furnished with immense statues, and arches connected all the rooms. In some places stairways gave access to the ramparts above.

The castle, like the carnival as a whole, was a tremendous success. Fifty thousand spectators attended its storming. Its fame continued beyond the life of the carnival. St. Paulites could not help chuckling when visitors to the Minnesota State Fair in September asked for directions to the ice palace.

1887

Like Montreal, St. Paul wanted to make each carnival more splendid than its predecessor. "This year the glories of last year will fade as does the moon before the stronger sun."[11]

The Sioux Indian village grew to one hundred inhabitants. The Carnival Association voted to hold two stormings of the ice palace and appropriated $3,500 for fireworks. "They will be such displays of pyrotechnics as the world never before dreamed

These stereoscopic pictures give us a glimpse inside a St. Paul ice palace. FACING

Various "ancient legends" account for the St. Paul ice palaces and the fireworks displays around them. King Borealis (on the left) journeyed from his far northern home to live in the ice castle during carnival time. NEAR RIGHT

The formation of snowshoe clubs, each with a distinctive costume, became epidemic. FAR RIGHT

St. Paul architect C. E. Joy (at far right) won a competition with his scheme for the 1887 ice palace. Joy, who had suggested to the Carnival Association that they bring in the Hutchisons from Montreal to design and build St. Paul's first ice castle, went on to design four magnificent ice palaces of his own.

The photograph, floor plan, and poster on these two pages all show Joy's St. Paul ice castle of 1887. A Gothic fantasy complete with flying buttresses, it was built in Central Park for $7,500. More than 42,000 square feet in area, it measured 217 feet by 194 feet. This palace's outstanding feature was its octagonal central tower, supported by walls 5 feet thick. Eight buttresses radiated from the tower, and its slender southeastern turret attained a height of 140 feet.

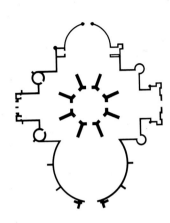

of.''[12] The city decked itself in festive garb: ''Eight miles of streets will be radiant with light, clusters of colored gas globes appearing every 50 feet, while at the junctions of the streets will be discovered graceful gas arches, or massive arches of evergreens, from among whose foliage gleam forth bright sparks of fire.''[13]

The cost of the ice palace increased to $7,500. St. Paul's architects competed for the two hundred dollar prize for the best design, and Charles E. Joy, who had recommended using Hutchison the year before, emerged as winner. Joy's first ice palace was a Gothic fantasy, complete with flying buttresses.

Again the castle went up in Central Park. More than 42,000 square feet in area, it measured 217 feet by 194 feet by 140 feet high. The blocks of ice composing it varied from 2 feet to 6 feet in length, from 12 inches to 18 inches in thickness.

The tower, octagonal in plan, 50 feet in diameter, rose from the building's center. Belt courses of projecting ''rock-ice'' traversed it at heights of 28 feet, 43 feet, 62 feet, and 80 feet. Eight buttresses radiated from the tower's outer angles. Each buttress was surmounted by a flying buttress, which reached up to a small flanking turret. Larger than the others, the southeastern turret extended 14 feet above the main tower. Its 140-foot height was the highest level attained by ice blocks in this palace, and this was surmounted by a flagpole 20 feet high. An amazing height! Five-foot-thick walls supported this wonderful tower.

Most visitors entered the ice palace from Summit Avenue, through an archway 16 feet wide and 15 feet high. Atop the arch sat a colossal statue of King Borealis, holding a colored electric light, supported on either side by a polar bear rampant. The wall of the arch was 9 feet thick.

The archway led to a circular enclosure 95 feet in diameter.

In the 1880s, electric light itself was still a novelty, and all the newspapers remarked on the lighting of each ice palace. Two hundred large electric lamps illuminated the 1887 St. Paul castle.

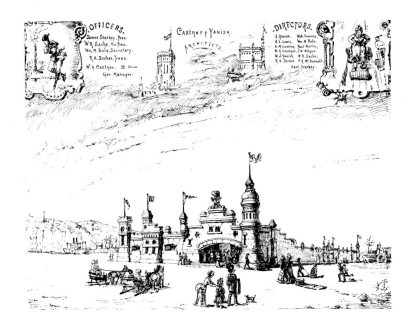

Three ice palaces loomed over wintry landscapes in 1887. In addition to Montreal's and St. Paul's, West St. Paul built a castle across the Mississippi River to demonstrate their rising prosperity.

Beyond this lay a rectangular courtyard (approximately 135 by 90 feet), in the center of which rose the main tower. The courtyard walls were 23 feet high. At each angle formed by the walls stood a tower, corniced and battlemented. Two were circular, two square. Beyond the central court, the ice palace terminated in an apse 60 feet in diameter. The rear entrance, an arch 8 feet in diameter, opened out of it.

Two side entrances approached the central yard through antechambers. Both entrances were double arches, 6 feet in width. Two square towers, tapering into circular turrets, flanked each entrance. Each tower was 47 feet high.

About 200 large electric lights lit the palace at night. ''The most gorgeous effect will be produced by the use of changeable globes of many brilliant hues.''[14] An extensive skating rink lay inside the palace, and many ice statues adorned the interior.

There was a massive representation of Bartholdi's "Liberty Enlightening the World."

The 1887 St. Paul Carnival boasted two ice palaces. The people of West St. Paul (located south of St. Paul on the other side of the Mississippi River) wanted to call attention to their own rapidly growing section of the city. Architects Castner & Yanish designed a charming facade with a 40-foot-high corner tower and a grand archway 24 feet wide. The walls enclosed a huge skating rink, 400 by 150 feet. A series of small rooms provided for visitors' comfort: a ladies' retiring room, a hot lunch room, a warming room complete with fireplace, an oyster room, a gentlemen's coat room, a gallery, and a bandstand. At the rear of the

Carnival derives, in part, from pagan agricultural festivals, in which the fertile forces of summer drove out the demons of winter. The devils, harlequins, and shaggy men of historical parades all grew out of these ancient winter demons. These "abominable snowmen" are preparing to set off from the 1888 St. Paul ice palace.

rink was a 900-foot-long toboggan slide. The castle cost about $2,000.

1888

The 1888 carnival featured a wedding, performed in the east room of the ice palace before 6,000 guests. The bridal couple, George G. Brown and Eva N. Evans, were escorted there by a

Lithographed by the H.M.Smyth Printing Co. St.Paul.   H.Bro Sill.   F.T.CANOLL. PUBLISHER.

From its opening day, the 1888 Carnival centered on C. E. Joy's second ice palace. Besides such usual diversions as ice skating and a Sioux Indian village, this carnival included a wedding, performed in the east room of the castle. A brass band on snowshoes provided music.

squadron of police, a marching band, the Pioneer Press Brigade and Drum Corps, and the Seven Corners Snowshoe Club. They took their vows on a dais under one of the arches of the ice palace, as a flare of red fire emblazoned the sky.

The carnival's Industrial Parade attracted 20,000 participants for a seven-mile march. One small town was represented by thirty floats. A local fish dealer passed out oysters on the half shell among the 200,000 viewers.

From its opening day, Wednesday, January 25, the carnival focused on C. E. Joy's magnificent second ice palace. This huge structure, replete with turrets, arches, sculpture, and battlements, covered about an acre. It measured 195 by 190 feet, and cost $7,000.

Work on the palace had begun December 19, 1887. The People's Ice company furnished the ice blocks, which were cut from Lake Como. Each block measured about 22 by 32 by 18 inches. The contractors, Messrs. Rhéaume & St. Pierre, assembled more than 55,000 blocks of ice into the finished building.

The palace's dominant central tower reached the rousing height of 130 feet. It began as a 50-foot square, with slender circular turrets at the corners. At the height of 80 feet, the main tower became a cylinder (with a diameter of 40 feet), and the turrets tapered into pinnacles.

The outer walls of the palace rose 30 feet. The main entrance lay beneath an arch 20 feet wide, guarded by circular turrets 60 feet high. Two smaller entrances, each with its own turrets,

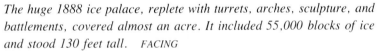

The huge 1888 ice palace, replete with turrets, arches, sculpture, and battlements, covered almost an acre. It included 55,000 blocks of ice and stood 130 feet tall.   *FACING*

This 2,000-foot-long toboggan slide ran down Ramsey Hill. Indian toboggans had been made of poplar and elder, lashed together with rawhide. St. Paulites glided on toboggans of durable ash and white oak, with the cross-bars screwed to the bottom.   *ABOVE*

''There is no sport played on ice or snow that does not find its hundreds of devotees during the weeks of riot and festival,'' explains The Northwest Magazine, *Here curlers compete in the foreground, while snowshoers march in the rear.*   *TOP, RIGHT*

Statues of ice were found both outside and within the 1888 palace. Five large niches carved in the front wall of the main tower held images of a polar bear, snowshoer, skater, tobogganer and curler.   *BOTTOM, RIGHT*

This very colorful Carnival edition of the 1889 St. Paul Dispatch *sold for twenty-five cents.*

pierced the building's sides. At the castle's back, the outer wall ballooned out to form a large circular courtyard.

Inside the palace, the visitor could admire the front wall of the main tower, in which five large niches had been carved. The uppermost one contained the figure of an immense polar bear; the others were adorned with statues of a snowshoer, skater, tobogganer, and curler.

The palace also housed a maze about 80 feet in diameter, situated at the northeast corner of the court walls. Five separate paths, separated by low walls of ice, led to the center of the puzzle, where circular stairs took the visitor out. Though not as intricate as Montreal's 1887 maze, it still provided a challenge.

The Burlington Free Press and Times explained that "... through the whole building run concealed pipes by which it can be brilliantly illuminated by electric light. With this slight exception the entire structure is of ice." [15]

The St. Paul and Minneapolis Pioneer Press described the completed castle: "The perfect translucency of the material of which the home of the Frost King is built, never showed to better advantage than on last evening. Though none but white lights were used, the effect was brilliant, for the difference in thickness of the blocks of ice gave the palace that delicately shaded appearance that art could not bring out." [16]

The Carnival Association had voted to hold three stormings of the ice palace. The first two ran according to plan, but on the day of the final storming, the temperature rose into the forties. An audience of 100,000 people surrounded a palace that had begun to melt. Worse still, the fireworks had been stored inside the building and many were too soggy to ignite. It was a dismal ending to a glorious enterprise!

1889 and 1890

C. E. Joy drew up plans for an 1889 ice palace, but the weather refused to cooperate. "Temperatures in the month of December

palace. A new site had been selected, on the west side of the Mississippi near the Wabasha Street Bridge. The scheme was asymmetrical; an imposing northern tower would have risen far above the rest of the building. The outworks would have been 320 feet by 315 feet, longer than those of any previous palace.

Although St. Paul tried to make the early carnivals important social events, it is doubtful that they achieved the easy international elegance of Montreal. Still, hearty Minnesota hospitality made the festivals extremely enjoyable, and skating parties were always part of the fun. On the left, a woman skates in front of the 1888 ice palace, temporary home of King Borealis (in the inset).

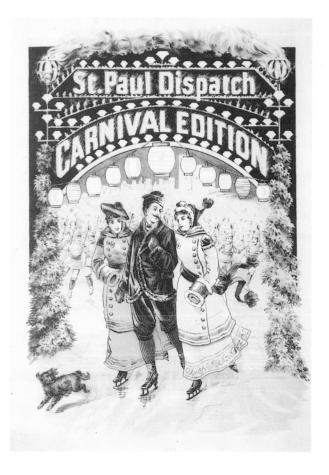

soared to the 60s; skies were balmy and precipitation was nil. On Christmas Day it was 23 above, and it was 33 above on New Year's Day.''[17] The January sunshine was so strong that the rivers and lakes "were as open as they'd been in July and it was impossible to cut any ice.''[18] When it did rain, the St. Paulites sloshed unhappily through the mud of unpaved streets.

The Carnival Association voted to postpone the festival until 1890. Unfortunately, that year temperatures again failed to sink to the required levels. By this time, the whole idea had lost momentum, and no more carnivals were planned for several years.

Descriptions and pictures remain of the unbuilt 1889-90 ice

The 1889 ice palace would have been larger than a football field, and its cylindrical tower would have topped 130 feet. Unfortunately, two warm winters in a row ended St. Paul's first period of intensive ice palace building.

According to the design, within these outer walls, 38 feet high, rose a second set of walls. Within the second walls stood the grand hall of the palace, 165 feet by 116 feet. The entire south end of the fortification formed a giant maze. The scheme also included a skating rink, restaurant, and dance floor.

The main tower rose from a 40-foot-square base. A cylindrical turret 20 feet in diameter stood at one of its corners. The square tower climbed to a height of 112 feet, the turret to 132.

The main entrance would have faced the bluff, and the entering visitor would have passed beneath a free-standing arch of ice, then marched up an esplanade 100 yards long.

1896

The carnival was revived in 1896 but only for that year. The program included curling, skating, and other winter sports. Parades have always been a major feature of St. Paul winter carnivals, and this year was no exception. A preliminary parade was held January 17. Uniformed marching clubs, such as the Red Men and the Elks, had become popular. Young ladies composed most of the Minnehaha Club.

The festivities centered around Fort Karnival, a stockade and frontier fort in ice. Captain Wilkinsop of Fort Snelling directed the erection of the ice fort in Aurora Park. Rhéaume & St. Pierre again secured the building contract. C. E. Joy did not participate; he was busy building a more elaborate ice palace in Leadville, Colorado (See Chapter 6).

Fort Karnival was meant to be 660 feet long by 300 feet wide, but the extremes of the front wall were abandoned due to the difficulty of building in a mild winter. The general design appeared long and low. The outer walls rose 15 feet; the corner towers 20 feet. The main entrance was an archway, between twin round towers both 25 feet high. Behind the entrance loomed a sally-port 35 feet in height. Chevaux de frise topped the wall, and an American flag ornamented each point.

Three different cities built ice palaces in 1896; Leadville, Québec, and St. Paul. This photograph and drawing show St. Paul's effort, Fort Karnival, a stockade and frontier fort of ice. Fort Karnival was meant to be 660 feet long by 300 feet wide, but a warm spell caused the builders to reduce the scheme. The sally-port behind the entrance was 35 feet high.

Standing on University Avenue directly opposite the main entrance to the fort the beautiful facade and retaining walls of the structure look like a fairy palace of crystal, lit up with millions of lights [that] shine and sparkle in prismatic glory. In the center is a mass of crystal towering high in the air, every inch of it glittering in the effort to permit the egress of the beams of light that fill all the space in the crystal chambers.[19]

Inside the fort were two toboggan slides and a coasting slide. The 200-yard toboggan slides ran in opposite directions, so

that enthusiasts could take one immeditely after the other. Fort Karnival also contained a village of two hundred Dakota Sioux Indians, "a first-class restaurant," and warming and retiring rooms.[20] A block house of ice, 60 feet by 50 feet by 25 feet high, was used as a fireworks manufacturing plant. The organizers scheduled the house for destruction, by explosion and fire, on January 30, the carnival's last day. Rain interfered, the fort dripped water like tears, and the final storming had to be postponed.

1916 and 1917

The carnival was revived again during these two years, largely due to the enthusiasm and financial contributions of Louis W. Hill, son of railroad tycoon James J. Hill.

The 1916 festival was distinguished by the selection of 108 queens, and by the introduction of the gasoline engine. Many of the new motorized floats broke down, and an order was passed banning them from the 1917 parade.

Twenty-one thousand persons—half the size of the entire regular United States Army at that time—were enrolled in carnival marching clubs in 1917. The most dramatic event of the carnival, however, was the 510-mile dog sled race. The contest-

Wealthy St. Paul citizen Louis W. Hill helped revive the carnival in 1916 and 1917. The plan of the 1917 ice fort was a Greek cross with an entrance at each end and a throne room in the center. The American entry into World War I ended the plans for a 1918 carnival.

ants drove their teams from Winnipeg, Canada, along the great Northern right-of-way. Albert Campbell, a Canadian Indian, won the race. Fred Hartman, the only American to enter, was hailed as a hero by the American press because he completed the race on foot, after his lead dog was killed.

The ice palaces of these years were modest efforts. In 1916, an ice fort was erected on Harriet Island. The "History of the St. Paul Winter Carnival" and the "Seventy-fifth Anniversary Souvenir Booklet" describe it as heart-shaped, but the 1916 Souvenir Booklet shows a rectangular enclosure, with 12-foot-high walls, surrounding an ice rink.

Rice Park provided the site for the 1917 ice fort. The fort's plan was a Greek cross with an entrance at each end and a throne room in the center. The outworks were about 10 feet high.

The American entry into World War I ended the plans for a 1918 carnival, and no more ice palaces were built in St. Paul until 1937. Their fame expanded in 1918, however, with the publication of F. Scott Fitzgerald's short story, "The Ice Palace."

5

Northern
Fortresses
Québec and Ottawa

Québec

Québec City, capital of the province of the same name, is the only fortified city in North America. French explorer Samuel de Champlain founded the city in 1608. Its name comes from an Algonquian word meaning "where the river narrows."[1] The wide St. Lawrence and the narrow St. Charles rivers frame Québec City, which forms a cape at their intersection. The terrain divides sharply; the upper cape rises about 200 feet above the lower. This dramatic setting, the ancient stone walls, and the large number of quaint old buildings make Québec a particularly charming city.

The largely Roman Catholic population of Québec had traditionally made merry before Lent, but in 1880 this "carnaval" began to grow in importance and intricacy. Statues of colored snow began appearing to decorate the intersections of streets. Sporting activities took place. Québec's citizens rode on toboggans and walked on showshoes; they raced their horses on the frozen St. Charles and crossed the cold St. Lawrence in canoes. (These canoe races have continued to the present time. Brave teams of sportsmen row when they can, but sometimes have to run across packs of ice, pushing and pulling their boats along with them.)

1894

The year 1894 was a time of trouble for some parts of the world: China and Japan went to war; Captain Alfred Dreyfus was unjustly convicted of treason in France; and 20,000 unemployed workers marched on Washington. In Québec, however, it was the year of the "most remarkable carnival of the nineteenth century."[2]

The Québec *Daily Telegraph* encouraged the idea of a major

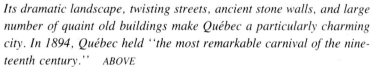

Its dramatic landscape, twisting streets, ancient stone walls, and large number of quaint old buildings make Québec a particularly charming city. In 1894, Québec held "the most remarkable carnival of the nineteenth century." *ABOVE*

Quebeckers expressed their carnival enthusiasm with constructions such as a mammoth snow ball (in 1896) and the giant beer bottle shown here. Visitors to the 1894 Carnival could enter the bottle, which stood roughly 50 feet tall. *TOP, RIGHT*

This Eiffel-tower-shaped living arch was built at the corner of St. Paul and Palace streets in 1894. Cheering snowshoers manned it when the Governor General and his lady passed beneath. Lord and Lady Aberdeen, who served as honorary patrons to the carnival, completely charmed the press. *BOTTOM, RIGHT*

Québec is the only fortified city in North America. Its first ice palace rose opposite Parliament, over a portion of the old city wall. At night arc lights brilliantly illuminated the ice fort and two detached towers.

carnival, and Lord Aberdeen, the Governor General of Canada, served as honorary patron. The carnival opened on January 26. "The streets were lined with sapins, and the houses were gay with flags and colored cotton. . . ."[3] Monuments of ice, carved by the wood sculptor Louis Jobin, adorned the streets. A huge beer bottle, roughly 50 feet tall, was constructed from blocks of ice. Five living arches were built in various parts of the city, and a little fort copied the one at Chateauguay. One citizen carved a handsome ice lion in front of his house.

The carnival was a great success. Among the many foreign visitors were Mr. and Mrs. John Jacob Astor, who stayed at the Chateau Frontenac. The residents of Québec themselves participated with enthusiasm. When Lord and Lady Aberdeen arrived in town on January 30, in the middle of a blinding blizzard, hundreds of snowshoers turned out to greet them. The governor general's train, "drawn by two powerful engines with a snowplow in front . . . looked like a moving mass of snow."[4]

An arch at the corner of St. Paul and Palace streets shaped like the Eiffel tower was manned by snowshoers who cheered and sang as their excellencies passed beneath it.

Carnival activities included concerts, student parades, performances of a Montreal opera troupe, a military review, a children's costume ball, and canoe races. Crowds gravitated to the maple sugar cabin, the Eskimo igloo, and the Huron Indian encampment. There was even a fancy dress masquerade at the Québec Skating Rink, where "Mrs. Astor wore a very handsome princess costume . . . "[5] and John Jacob Astor went as Louis XIV.

The newspapers devoted admiring attention to the words and deeds of Lord and Lady Aberdeen. The Montreal *Gazette* reported that, during the blizzard, "Lord Aberdeen remarked that they sometimes had weather like this in Scotland."[6] When the curlers discovered that the Governor General was also a player, they induced him to join in a match. Another incident demonstrates the tremendous difference in attitude between 1894 and

Very much a fortress, the 1894 ice palace measured 120 feet by 50 feet. Outworks and circular turrets guarded the 63-foot-tall central tower.

the present time. In the torchlight parade that followed the ice palace storming, Lord and Lady Aberdeen rode in the Levis Club float. The float was a facsimile locomotive, driven by a veteran engineer. Lady Aberdeen astonished the engineer by addressing him "in pure Parisian French. As he said himself when he had recovered from his amazement, she spoke French better than he did."[7]

The carnival closed with the Tandem Club drive on February 3. About fifty smart teams paraded along the chosen route. Two senior citizens drove their ancient caleche, built in 1700, while a newly married couple rode in an old berlin. Although elegant, the drive was not entirely placid. A team of horses went out of control and injured three people.

Québec's first ice palace rose opposite Parliament, over a portion of the old city wall. On the Grand Allée, just outside the St. Louis gate, a visitor could see a very grand scene. On one side arc lights brilliantly illuminated the ice fort and two detached towers, while on the other every window of the Parliament buildings, from the cellar to the top of the tower, blazed with light.

This palace was very much a fortress. Outworks and circular turrets girded a tall central tower, square in plan. The building measured 120 feet by 50 feet by 63 feet high. Berlinquet and Raymond designed it; Cummings and Sharp constructed it.

The highlight of the carnival occurred on February 2, when the ice palace was stormed. Snowshoers, soldiers, and Indians—Huron and Montagnais—participated in the mock battle. Some defended the structure, while others attacked it. They fought with torches and fireworks—the fireworks budget was about $2,000. Nearly 2,500 snowshoers, from Québec, Montreal, Levis, Sherbrooke, Fraserville, and Burlingon, Vermont, took part in the display. Brilliant lights glowed through the transparent fort and towers in constantly changing colors. "At one time they would show a bright red, then green, then blue, and, in fact, all the colors of the rainbow."[8]

Québec's residents were very proud of this carnival. *L'Union Libérale* proclaimed, on February 3, 1894:

With energy, good will, and, especially, skill, we can do here what others do . . . [By "others," the writer surely means the people of Montreal] . . . The ice palace, the numerous living arches scattered in our streets, the pretty statues, attest not only to the work but also to the

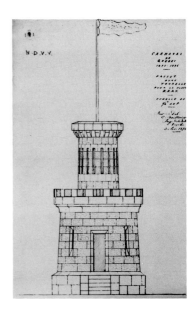
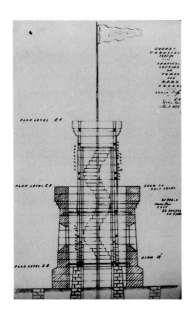

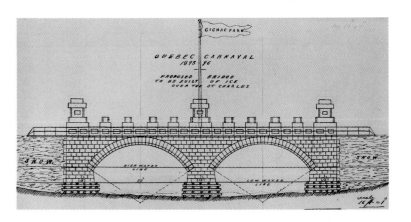

Although this design may never have been built, another kind of "ice bridge" was in place for the 1896 Carnival. The river in front of Québec City froze over. (Elevation of proposed ice bridge over St. Charles River) BOTTOM, LEFT

Ice forts, towers, and statues went up all over Québec City before the carnivals. (Elevation and section of proposed tower, 1895–96) TOP, RIGHT AND FAR RIGHT

This plaza included an Eskimo igloo at the center of a maze, a maple sugar cabin, and a souvenir shop. (Site plan) MIDDLE, RIGHT

artistic taste of our population. We still remain the intellectual center of the country, the Athens of Canada.

1896

In 1896, Guglielmo Marconi received the first wireless patent from Britain, and William McKinley defeated William Jennings Bryan for president of the United States. This was the only year in which major ice palaces were built in three different cities: Leadville, St. Paul, and Québec. The citizens of Québec erected an extremely distinctive building, a conical ziggurat of ice.

The Carnival Committee was not immune to the usual ambition of carnival planners: "Quebeckers have been so proud of their success in the carnival of 1894, that they determined to exceed all former efforts in 1896."[9]

The inhabitants expressed their enthusiasm with various constructions. A mammoth snowball, on the old Upper Town Market Place, grew to 50 feet in diameter. The firemen at the Central Station built a model of Montmorenci Falls, complete with water flowing over it. Another fire station put up a 40-foot windmill in blocks of colored ice. One snow fort rose to a height of 50 feet. "Snow forts and ice castles are being erected on all sides. . . . Triumphal arches will also be seen in great profusion, one of the most magnificent being situated on the corner of St. Joseph and Crown streets. It is quadrilateral in shape, and tops the surrounding tall stores."[10] More than 500 laborers worked on official carnival constructions. A spiral slide, designed by M. Baillarge, the city engineer, unfortunately was not built. It would have been "the Carnival gem in point of sport," said the engineer sadly.[11]

Visiting celebrities differed from those of 1894. The arrival of Madame Albani, the Canadian prima donna, thrilled Quebeckers, but the Governor General and Lady Aberdeen disappointed them by canceling their visit, on account of the death of Prince Henry of Battenburg.

In 1896, the Quebeckers erected this distinctive conical ziggurat of ice. Like the 1885 Montreal condora, this ice palace took its inspiration from the Tower of Babel. It rose, in three tiers, to a height of 100 feet.

Sleighs of all kinds glided in the Allegorical Drive: "The fire brigade, with reels, engines, etc., and a house on fire, led off. The Québec Bicycle Club, with a toboggan drawn by mounted wheelmen, followed, and then came the C. P. R. employees with a full size engine and snow plough; some twenty-five of the employees, all dressed as Mephistopheles, followed it."[12]

The problem of crime was handled simply in 1896. On the second day of the carnival, a lady complained that her pocket had been picked of seventeen dollars. The next day the police ordered two suspicious characters out of town.

Lieutenant Governor Chapleau opened the ice palace on January 27, surrounded by immense crowds of spectators. Set on the old city wall, on the same site as the fortress of 1894, it measured roughly 60 feet in diameter at its base. The spiral tower rose, in three tiers, to a height of 100 feet. The two lower tiers were of ice, the top one, snow. A spiral staircase wound around the building, and a ball and flag topped it off.

The carnival ended on January 31, with the storming of this conical fortress of ice. Files of snowshoers marched and advanced on the palace with colored torches and fireworks. The fireworks display, which cost $2,000, "exceeded, in beauty, that of the last Carnival."[13] A torchlight parade followed the storming. "The display was witnessed by thousands of people, and all who saw it are loud in its praise."

Ottawa

The national capital of Canada, Ottawa was founded in 1827. The city is located at the point where the Ottawa River tumbles over the Chaudière Falls. Two other rivers flow in downstream: the Gatineau and the Rideau. One man-made waterway joins them, the Rideau Canal, built for defense at the suggestion of the original Duke of Wellington.

Ottawa's dramatic natural setting inspired its splendid Parliament Buildings. On a bluff overlooking the Ottawa River, these three stone Gothic buildings lift their green copper roofs and spires to the skies. Two architects who worked on these buildings—A. C. Hutchison and King Arnoldi—later designed ice palaces as well.

By 1895, Ottawa had long since progressed from a brawling lumber town to a sophisticated metropolis. Located in Ontario just across the Ottawa River from Québec Province, Ottawa combines English and French customs. This bridging character was one of the reasons why Queen Victoria proclaimed it Canada's capital. It seems appropriate that Ottawa became the only English Canadian city to adopt the custom, originated in French Canada, of holding a winter carnival with an ice palace.

1895

In the year that Roentgen discovered X-rays, Ottawa held its first winter carnival. Like every other nineteenth-century city that ever planned such an enterprise, Ottawa had high hopes. "The intention is to make this the greatest winter festival ever held in Canada."[14]

The Ottawans turned their city into a festive capital. They decorated nearly all of the businesses and public buildings handsomely with bunting, flags, or evergreens, and many with lights. A living arch was built on MacKenzie Avenue. Two citizens erected an arch on Lyon Street from ice and evergreens. Its ice abutments, 15-feet high, supported a 40-foot span of evergreens. A restaurateur built an ice pyramid, 18-feet high, hollow and illuminated, in front of his establishment. The smallest notable structure was a model of the ice castle in sugar. Pastry cook A. H. Bertschinger prepared this 3-foot-high delicacy as a carnival decoration for the Russell House, the city's most elegant hotel.

The carnival opened January 21. Activities included skating, snowshoeing, tobogganing, bowling competitions, a grand torchlight procession, a national concert, an allegorical drive, and a masque ball. Thousands of visitors came, from other parts of

Architect King Arnoldi designed the 1895 Ottawa ice palace. Like A. C. Hutchison, Arnoldi launched his career by working on Ottawa's splendid Parliament buildings.   ABOVE, LEFT

Set on Nepean Point, the 1895 ice palace had a working drawbridge. When the carnival construction committee ran short of money, they decided to build the palace's main tower out of wood.   ABOVE, RIGHT

Canada and from the United States. In New York City, the New York Central Railroad provided travelers with the special excursion rate of $14.50 to Ottawa and back, just for the carnival.

The New York Times announced on January 18: "Well-known society people of New York and Brooklyn have signified their intention of making the trip." Although the governors of New York and Vermont sent their regrets, the carnival ball at the Russell House was a splendid success. Visitors came from

Montreal, Québec, Sudbury, and Toronto in Canada, and from Cleveland, Chicago, Detroit, and New York in the States. Mayor Borthwick and Sir James Grant danced in the quadrille of honor. Some of the ladies' outfits sound as lovely as they must have looked: one of the mayor's daughters wore garneted cactus silk, with point lace trimmings, while the other wore Coquelicot Shanghai silk trimmed with heavy Parisian lace.

Another setting for carnival enjoyment was the ice palace, constructed on Nepean Point, a high bluff overhanging the Ottawa River. This icy fortress measured roughly 130 by 30 feet, and it had a working portcullis. The tower on the east corner reached about 40 feet in height.

The ice palace was designed by King Arnoldi, chairman of the carnival construction committee. His firm, Arnoldi & Calderon, drew up plans for the building and supervised its construction. Born in Ottawa in 1843, Arnoldi apprenticed as an architect in Montreal. At the start of the construction of the Parliament Buildings, he returned to Ottawa and worked with the firm of Fuller and Jones. By 1895, Arnoldi had practiced architecture for thirty-five years.

In December of 1894, it looked as though Arnoldi's ice castle design would never be realized. The contract for construction originally was awarded to W. Kilt, who had promised to assemble 80,000 cubic feet of ice into a fortress at a cost of only $1,925. By December 28, Kilt had abandoned this difficult commitment.

The construction committee looked around for a substitute scheme or builder that would not unbalance their budget. They considered a suggestion that they build a castle of rough wood, decorate it with brush, and apply a stream of water to freeze over it. Alum water, sprinkled over afterwards, would have made the palace glisten. This wooden castle would have been cheap to build and could have been dramatically burned in the final storming. (Ice-palace lovers, however, would have been heartbroken.)

In the end, the committee came up with a feasible compound scheme. They reduced the size of the plan slightly and incorporated some wood. The main portion of the palace would be built of ice (at a cost of $1,540), while the big tower would be built of wood, covered with cedar bows, and frozen over (at a cost of $600). Richard Lester, one of the best known contractors in town, agreed to take the whole job for $2,140.

Soon Lester had about 100 men and 45 horses working on the ice palace. Some of the workers were cutting and carting ice (about 1,000 blocks a day) from the Rideau River. "Many judges of ice say that the quality is better than that obtained above the Chaudière Falls [on the Ottawa River]. It is of a delicate blue tint and looks remarkably pretty."[15]

On Nepean Point, the rest of Lester's force assembled the castle. Two derricks pulled the large blocks (about 20 inches by 15 inches by 40 inches) up the walls. Lester personally directed the placement of each block of ice.

A stream of fascinated visitors interfered with the rapid work. The committee finally reduced their numbers—and raised some money—by charging admission to the site. Pedestrians paid five cents; admission for a rig was twenty-five cents.

The finished ice palace revealed its compound nature at night, when about a dozen arc lamps lit it up from the inside. The icy part glowed a mellow color, throwing the big wooden tower into gloomy relief. The Ottawa *Journal* voiced one criticism. They suggested that the castle committee sprinkle the castle floor with sand or ashes, because the "inside of the building is rough, slippery and dangerous to limb."[16]

Although not outstanding in size or design, the 1895 Ottawa ice fortress inspired splendid pomp. The Chaudière Falls and the Parliament Buildings were illuminated every night. The torchlight parade, according to the *Burlington Free Press*, "surpassed anything ever seen in Montreal."[17]

Guns, as well as fireworks, played a role in the storming of the ice palace on January 25. The Ottawa Field Battery opened the attack. Then brigades of snowshoers advanced across the frozen Ottawa River. A large searchlight from the Parliament tower lit up their path. The defense answered by firing the heavy guns at Nepean Point, just in front of the ice castle. While the attacking party used ropes and ladders to scale the cliffs,

the rattle of musketry was added to the crashing booms of the batteries. The fires of rockets and roman candles from the snowshoers and the flaring firework displays from the castle fairly filled the air with sparks and streams of fire. Colored fires and electrical illuminating effects transformed the castle into a palace of fire. The snowshoe brigades re-formed at the top of the cliff and made a grand final rush up on the castle amid myriad sparks and blazing lights. The blowing up and burning of the castle was very realistic. Then all the lights went out at once and some beautiful prismatic illuminations formed the finale.[18]

1904

In 1904, Russia and Japan were at war, and the New York subway opened. That year saw neither ice palace nor winter carnival, but the achievement of Ottawan Constable Carey is worthy of mention. This gentleman singlehandedly erected a large fortress of snow on the Rideau Hall grounds. (Rideau Hall, also known as Government House, is the official residence of Canada's Governor General.) "The frozen fort is probably the biggest ever built outside those that have figured in winter carnivals."[19]

Cold weather, an abundance of snow, and a two-hour break between his periods of duty gave Constable Carey the opportunity to accomplish his Herculean labor. A former member of the Royal Irish constabulary, he patterned the fort after Castle Antrim in Ireland.

After two weeks' work, Constable Carey had completed everything but the finishing touches. The building measured 40 feet by 30 feet. The main wall was 25 feet high, the main tower 30 feet in height. "It will be embellished with parapet and ornate trimmings such as are found on all well-built castle fortresses. When illuminated from the interior, the snow fort should present a unique and beautiful appearance. The Earl and Countess of Minto have evinced interest in the building of the snow fort, which stands directly in front of Government House."[20]

1922

In the Roaring Twenties, while people argued about whether jazz was the latest, greatest thing or a sign of cultural decay, Ottawa decided to have a dizzy, dazzling week and host the Canadian National Winter Carnival. The Ottawans marked 1922 with an ice palace, an ice column, and a special toboggan slide. Flags, streamers, and other decorations appeared on Sparks and Elgin streets.

The Governor General and his wife, Lord and Lady Byng of Vimy, opened the carnival on January 28. Activities included a Mardi Gras ball, boxing, hockey, speed and fancy skating, moccasin dancing, hobby horse hockey, snowshoeing and skiing, wrestling, horse racing, torchlight parades, and an exciting election for Queen of the Carnival. This was not a free election—citizens became eligible to cast votes by buying tickets, and they could buy as many as they wished.

A party of Mohawk Indians and brigades of snowshoers supplied color and pageantry. The two Ottawa snowshoe clubs wore neatly contrasting costumes: members of the older Gaieté Club sported white blanket cloth suits with blue trimmings, and tuques, sashes, and stockings of royal blue, while those in the new Freiman Club marched in royal blue trimmed with white.

At the Mardi Gras, cash prizes of twelve dollars each were awarded for the best lady's and the best man's costumes. At St. Patrick's Hall, every afternoon and evening during Carnival Week, orchestras played "the dreamiest of the dream kind waltzes, the tum-tum, finger snapping, peppy one-steps and the happy, snappy, jazzy, bluesy fox trots."[21]

Theresa McCadden, who won the election for Carnival Queen, was introduced to her subjects at a ball at Laurier House. (This mansion, built in 1878, was named after one of its occupants, Sir Wilfred Laurier, Canadian Prime Minister from 1896 to 1911.) Mohawk Indians, wearing war paint, brandishing tomahawks, and uttering piercing cries, enlivened the ball with a dance.

Three structures distinguished the carnival. Tall, slender, and glowing, the illuminated ice column rose 40 feet high on the Plaza Square. At the top perched a crown, used in 1901 on a visit to Ottawa by the then Duke of York, later King George V.

Ottawans built an impressive toboggan slide beside Laurier House. The "Slide-a-Mile" chute was thrilling and popular. Only one accident is reported: little Gazido Sito stuck out his foot and broke it. After this unhappy incident, the attendants took more care to instruct beginners in how to sit during "the joyous descent."[22]

The ice palace went up in Cartier Square. At night powerful searchlights played upon its medieval turrets and "lent it the brilliancy of a blue white diamond.''[23] The building was about 125 feet long and 65 feet high. ''The interior will be brilliantly and beautifully lighted with thousands of vari-colored lights.''[24]

W. G. Adamson served as contractor for both the ice palace and the Slide-a-Mile. W. E. Noffke, who designed the toboggan slide, may also have designed the castle.

On February 3, the last day of the carnival, the largest crowd in Ottawa history assembled in and around Cartier Square. The fireworks display lasted over an hour. ''Great flares were lighted at the top of each of the [palace's] four towers, accompanied by realistic lighting effects and the thunder of guns.''[25] Despite this

splendid show, the 1922 Ottawa ice palace was the only ice palace never successfully stormed: ''There was to have been a finale with an attack on the ice palace by the members of the snowshoe clubs, who were to advance against the grim walls from behind a barrage of fire, but the crowds broke through the roped area and prevented the attack being launched. So the castle still stands ready to resist the assault of any storming party.''[26]

———————————————

About 125 feet long and 65 feet high, this 1922 Ottawa castle was the only ice palace never successfully stormed. Disorderly crowds broke through the ropes meant to restrain them and aborted the attack.

St. Paul architect C. E. Joy traveled to Leadville, Colorado, to build this vast 1896 ice palace. Lovely though it looks, the palace was incomplete. It is ironic that three cities erected ice palaces in a year when unseasonably warm weather interfered with construction in both Leadville and St. Paul.

6

The
Leadville
Palace

1896

At an altitude of 10,188 feet, Leadville, Colorado, is the nation's highest incorporated city. The "cloud city" got its start as a mining town. The first prospectors entered a vast area of pine trees, brush, willows, and wild animals. Before the arrival of the prospectors, humans had inhabited the forest only in summer, when some Indians used it as recreational grounds.

Then called "Oro City," Leadville played a part in the 1859 gold rush. Houses and mines replaced parts of the wilderness. After the gold mines ran out, discoveries of lead and silver revitalized Leadville in 1877. By the end of 1894, miners had drawn more than $200,000,000 worth of different ores from the eastern side of the city.

The great panic of 1893 ended the boom. The repeal of the Sherman Silver Purchase Act caused the price of the white metal to plummet. In 1895, the Leadville economy was still shaking. Although the hills cradled abundant deposits of metal, it was not worth the cost of mining and smelting them. Men were out of work, laid off by the great mines and smelters. Prospectors could not get grubstakes. Even the denizens of the once-prosperous whorehouse row had begun to depart, taking their booty with them.[1]

In an effort to keep Leadville on the map, a group of saloon-keepers, gamblers, and other local businessmen decided to attract tourists with a winter-long Ice Carnival. E. W. Senior helped to start the Crystal Carnival Association, but Tingley S. Wood soon replaced him as president. Wood raised more than $40,000 from the sale of stock in the association.

The carnival gave Leadville society an opportunity to prove itself. The citizens of Leadville had always lived under the social shadow of Denver. "'People in the valleys are beginning to

Leadville, Colorado, was a rough and tumble mining town in the nine-teenth century, but the panic of 1893 closed many mines. In an effort to keep Leadville on the map, a group of saloon-keepers, gamblers, and other local businessmen decided to attract tourists with a winter-long ice carnival. ABOVE, LEFT

This lithograph shows Joy's original conception of the ice palace. The twin front towers, meant to be 90 feet tall, appear to have reached only about 60 feet in the actual building. ABOVE, RIGHT

realize that Leadville is something more than a rude mining camp. The cloud city has made her entree, at last, into society circles.' Class at last. Unfortunately, Lou Bishop was arrested by Officer Johnson a few days after Leadville made 'her entree' because he rode his horse through Scholtz's Saloon.''[2]

More conventional carnival activities included curling con-tests, skating competitions, tugs of war, and hockey tournaments. A toboggan slide was built, 2,100 feet long. Unique to the Lead-ville carnival was the rock drilling contest, in which local miners and teams from other Western mining camps participated. Other original competitions included those for the best impersonations of Grover Cleveland, a typical miner, a ''French maid,'' and an Irish biddy.''[3]

The Carnival Association commissioned St. Paul architect C. E. Joy to build the palace. He arrived in Leadville on November 6, 1895. The Carnival Association had already ac-quired five acres of land and had begun to clear them of forest. The site was on Capitol Hill between West Seventh and Eighth streets.

The Leadville Palace was probably Joy's most challenging commission in ice, for three reasons. The Carnival Association wanted the largest ice palace ever built, as well as a permanent wooden pavilion inside the ice structure, to be reused in subsequent years. Finally, since they were planning a winter-long carnival, the palace had to be ready by Christmas. Most previous winter carnivals had opened in late January or early February, allowing their builders a longer period of cold weather construction time.

Approximately 250 to 350 men (each earning from $2.50 to $3.50 per day) worked on the palace. Coble and Kerr, local contractors, supervised the interior woodwork, the erection of the steel girders, and the laying of the ice. At the Arkansas River, Turquoise Lake, Palmer Lake, and other lakes, workmen sawed ice into blocks and hauled it by team and sled to the construction site. Twenty teams were employed to haul the ice.

James A. Murray, foreman in charge of the actual labor on the ice palace, recalls: "At first we employed stone cutters to trim the ice blocks, but these proved much too slow, so we imported a number of Canadian wood choppers, who with their broad-axes did the work with neatness and dispatch. In the walls and towers we used 5000 tons of ice."[4]

Construction lurched haltingly along. The December weather was freakishly warm for the Leadville area, complete with the "chinook"—a warm, dry wind that descends the eastern slopes of the Rocky Mountains. On December 12, the temperature had risen to 65 degrees Fahrenheit. The ice the men were handling melted faster than they could lay it, and the wind cut crevices in the walls of the structure. Huge lengths of muslin and canvas were draped over the walls to shade them. Fortunately, the temperature dropped below freezing every night, and the evening crews made some progress. At night the fire department sprayed the palace with water, to fill in the cracks and seal the blocks together.

The chinook boded ill for the construction crew. While the wind took its course, the ginpole (block and tackle) used to lift the ice blocks broke and fell. One man, Sam Olds, received severe injuries. At about the same time, one of the northen towers collapsed, overthrowing a derrick. Two men who had been working on it fell some distance to the ground, but luckily escaped harm.

The ice palace opened on New Year's Day, 1896, with a costume parade in the afternoon and skating and dancing in the evening. More than 2,500 people visited the castle on opening day.

The palace was roughly cruciform in plan. According to the "Leadville Crystal Carnival" souvenir brochure, the long axis stretched 435 feet, the shorter axis 325 feet, and the tallest towers rose 90 feet. Sources give the dimensions of the ice blocks as either 5 feet by 2 feet by 22 inches or as 20 inches by 30 inches. The thickness of the palace walls is variously described as 5 feet or 8 feet.

Veils of mystery shroud the cost of the Leadville ice palace. "Nothing ever appeared in print that could be considered a complete accounting of the Leadville Crystal Carnival Association, nor have the corporation's records ever been found."[5] Estimates of the price range from $35,000 (according to O'Keefe & Stockdorf, Official Photographers for the Ice Palace Association) to over $140,000 (according to D. Longwell, in "The Leadville Ice Palace"). Even the lower figure is roughly ten times the cost of any previous ice palace.

The tallest towers, octagonal in plan and 40 feet in diameter, stood at the building's main north entrance. A comparison of Joy's design drawings with photographs of the actual ice palace reveals that these octagonal cylinders were never completed as planned. Although the "Leadville Crystal Carnival" reports that they rose 90 feet, inspection of the photographs indicates that they only attained a height of 50 to 60 feet. After missing the original Christmas deadline, the builders left the towers' second tiers severely truncated. An impression of completion was obtained, however, by topping each corner of the towers with a pinnacle.

Circular south towers, 40 feet in diameter, were designed to rise 60 feet above ground, but may actually have been somewhat shorter. Four smaller round towers pinned the corners of the main building.

According to the "Leadville Crystal Carnival," "From the north to the south towers the distance is 325 feet." At the southern end of the building lay an extension enclosing a merry-go-round. An ice arch, large enough to permit Seventh-Street traffic to pass beneath it, connected the "riding gallery" to the main building.

On Eighth Street, just outside the main northern entrance, rose "Leadville." This 31-foot-high ice statue depicted a woman standing on a pedestal and pointing east, "to the rich mineral hills from whence Leadville's wealth is taken."[6]

Eight wooden trusses supported the roof that covered the palace's main building. "Every inch of timber or iron was covered with 'ice frosting' to make the roof look like a bed of diamonds."[7] The largest central room, 190 feet by 80 feet, served as a skating rink. Ice arcades enclosed it on three sides. The arches rested on octagonal pillars, 5 feet in diameter and 15 feet apart. Incandescent electric lamps had been placed in the hollow center of each pillar and shone brightly through the transparent ice.

Passing through the eastern arcade, you came to the grand ballroom, 80 feet by 50 feet. The western arcade led to a room of equal size, which served as an auxiliary ballroom, dining hall,

The Leadville ice palace was the largest ever attempted. Roughly cruciform in plan, it stretched longer than a football field in both directions.
RIGHT

Part of the palace was a wooden-roofed pavilion, designed to be permanent. The central skating rink, see plan, was flanked by heated wood-and-glass ballrooms. Both ice skates and shoes twirled to the music of bands that performed from a balcony above the rooms.
FACING

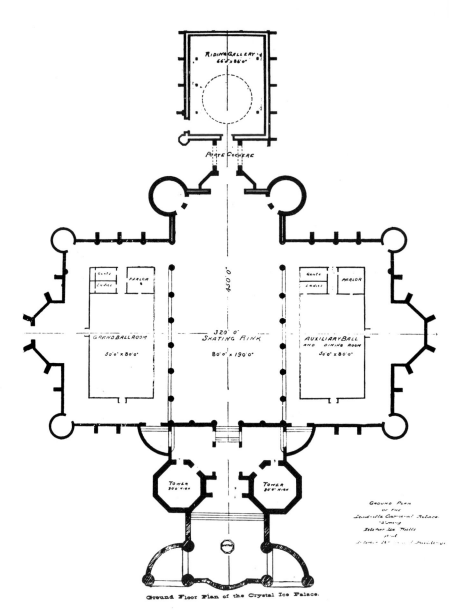

Ground Floor Plan of the Crystal Ice Palace.

and souvenir emporium. These two ballrooms were separate, heated wooden structures within the ice palace; glass panels allowed dancers and skaters to view each other. Each ballroom held three smaller rooms: a parlor, and separate dressing rooms for ladies and for gentlemen. The fifty-cents admission fee included the services of ladies' maids. Both ice skates and shoes twirled to the lively strains of the Fort Dodge Cowboy Band, who performed from a balcony between the rink and the grand ballroom.

Joy and Wood designed a series of ice statues for the palace, depicting the life of a successful miner. The palace walls served as exhibition space: displays of beer, stuffed animals, flowers, fruit, and many other products and decorative items were frozen into the walls.

Magnificent as the palace was, it did not draw in the anticipated number of visitors, and those who came did not spend money lavishly. In addition, the weather continued to frustrate every reasonable expectation. A thaw began to melt the palace in the early days of March. An unseasonable snow damped down the fireworks at the "Farewell Fete" on March 28. Finally, a volatile miners' strike claimed the public's full attention, and no new carnivals were ever planned in Leadville.

NIGHT SCENE
ST. PAUL WINTER SPORTS CARNIVAL 1937
(30,000 CAKES OF ICE IN BUILDING)

7

Crystal Pavilions: Modern St. Paul

In 1936, while Germany occupied the Rhineland and civilian unemployment in the United States stood at about seventeen percent, St. Paul decided to revive its winter carnival. Poor economic conditions do not seem to discourage winter carnivals. On the contrary, city merchants often plan these festivals when business needs stimulation. As the panic of 1893 led to the Leadville ice palace, so the stock market crash of 1929 led to the ice palaces of 1937 to 1947 in St. Paul. The carnival renaissance provided a welcome distraction from the Depression, and Works Progress Administration workers helped build the palaces.

St. Paul merchants decided that a winter carnival would spark business. While work crews finished the first St. Paul ice palace since 1917, a crowd of 100,000 people gathered.

The 1937 ice palace can be analyzed as a single wall, modulated in height and thickness. This building launched an ice palace renaissance, and bold Art Deco castles glistened in the years from 1937 to 1947.

The ice palaces of 1937 to 1947 were a series of marvelous Art Deco pavilions. Although not as tall as the three great early palaces, they were comparable in extent. At night electric lights illuminated these crystal palaces in patterns of changing color. Most of them were designed by the team of Charles A. Bassford, city architect, and his assistant, C. W. Wigington.

1937

Great excitement greeted the 1937 carnival, which secured crooner Rudy Vallee as its entertainment star. Such huge crowds jammed the streets for the torchlight parade that the marchers had to detour from their assigned route. Asked to play for an indoor parade a few days after the chaotic torchlight procession, Vallee replied: ''Swell. I'll give 'em all the march music they want—and the way they like it, for as long as they want it. It will be a big break for yours truly, too, for I didn't get a peep at Saturday night's parade, and I'd like to see some carnival uniforms and some marching!"[1]

The ice palace also caused quite a stir. While work crews put in a sixteen-hour day to finish the building, a crowd of 100,000 people gathered around the site. Twenty-thousand automobiles choked the approaches to the palace. Some of the vehicles carried license plates from Wisconsin, North and South Dakota, and Iowa. "Many of the visitors said they had traveled hundreds of miles for the sole purpose of seeing the building."[2]

Zero and subzero weather caused an addition to the usual building steps. Huge log fires blazed in the building all during construction. They heated eight 50-gallon oil drums filled with water. This hot water was used to cement the ice cakes together as they were laid on the walls. In the extremely cold weather, the water had to be kept near the boiling point or it would freeze as it was hoisted to the top of the wall.

Erected opposite the State Capitol, the ice palace measured about 193 feet in length, 86 feet at its widest point, and 60 feet in height. It used 30,000 ice cakes. Much simpler than the early castles, it can be analyzed as a single ice wall, modulated in height and thickness. This wall wrapped around three spaces, a central hall (128 feet by 55 feet) and two antechambers (22 feet by 22 feet, each). The wall's changing width created dramatic effects of translucency, opacity, and shadow. It varied in thickness from 6 feet 5 inches to 2 feet 9 inches, except at the main entrances, where it swelled to 15 feet 7 inches.

These thick entrances supported the building's greatest heights, peaks of 60 feet. Fifteen-foot-tall flagpoles capped these peaks. The palace's floor plan was symmetrical along both the longitudinal and transverse axes. The main northeastern facade was repeated on the southwestern side of the building; the two side elevations matched each other.

As is customary, the ice palace was destroyed after the carnival ended. Small charges of dynamite placed at various points on the foundation shook the castle to pieces. The resulting pile of

ice was left to melt in the spring. Architect Bassford, who designed the building, explained that "it would be dangerous to allow the palace to melt by itself, as it would be impossible to keep watch continuously to prevent visitors going into the building while it was weakened by thawing."[3]

1938

The 1938 Carnival introduced an airplane to guide traffic during the grand parade.

The "ice palace" that year was eminently simple, consisting only of a facade and a skating rink. A sudden January thaw undermined the walls to such an extent that the builders stopped work and decided to blast down the facade as a safety precaution. "Three hours later an oldtime blizzard swept in out of the northwest, dropped the mercury 50 degrees overnight—and dramatically saved the castle."[4]

Two semicircular disks composed the facade of the completed palace. One stood 60 feet high, the other 50 feet high. Their brilliant lighting consumed as much electricity in ten days as a town of 7,000 inhabitants normally required in a year.

In front of the semicircles stretched a "mirror of ice," about 300 feet by 100 feet, over which skaters glided. Along both sides of the rink ran colonnades of ice, topped with 30-foot poles flying pennants. Jack Horner chaired the committee that designed the complex. Construction, in Dayton's Bluff, took about a week.

This "Ice Court" was chosen for construction over two more elaborate earlier designs. Scheme A, entitled "Windsor Castle," followed the tradition of the grand ice palaces of the previous century. It measured about 300 feet by 205 feet. The main octagonal tower (40 feet in diameter) rose from the rear wall to a height of 64 feet. Four square corner towers (either 32 feet by 32 feet or 40 feet by 40 feet) reached heights of 50 feet each. Twin slender octagonal towers (each 60 feet high) flanked the main southern entrance. A row of four small octagonal towers stood along each of the building's two side facades. The walls were 3 feet 8 inches thick. Inside the palace, a huge arena would have measured 273 feet by 140 feet.

Scheme B, "Fort Belvedere," also remained unbuilt. Similar in size and style to Scheme A, Scheme B had fewer towers (seven instead of fifteen) and an asymmetrical plan. It measured 312 feet by 190 feet. The tallest tower, octagonal in plan (35 feet in diameter), would have risen to a height of 67 feet.

1939

The 1939 Winter Carnival introduced the Battle Creek ski slide, where jumping competitions were held. The red-uniformed band that stormed the ice palace that year included Warren Burger, now Chief Justice of the U.S. Supreme Court. Newsreel crews from Paramount, Universal, Pathé, Fox, and Metro-Goldwyn-Mayer all came to St. Paul to film the festivities.

The castle, based on plans described in the *Arabian Nights*, was a gingerbread fantasy with slits, scallops, arched entrances, and three towers with tapered tops. Approximately 240 feet in length, it varied tremendously in width. A fanciful central tower measured about 80 feet high at its peak. The octagonal northern tower (35 feet in diameter) rose 50 feet high. The circular southern tower also measured 35 feet in diameter and 50 feet in height.

The palace rose near the lake in Como Park. Two hundred

The 1938 "ice palace" was eminently simple, consisting only of a facade and a skating rink. The two semicircular disks stood 50 and 60 feet high.

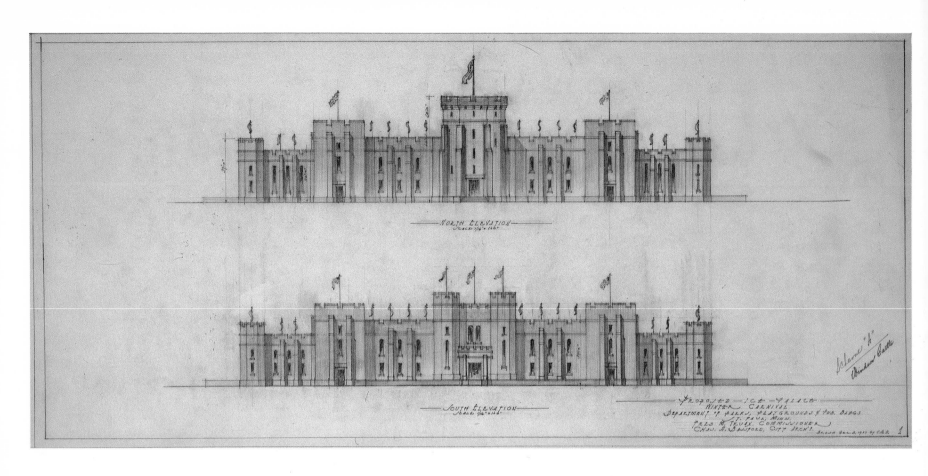

NORTH ELEVATION

SOUTH ELEVATION

The 1938 ice court was chosen for construction rather than two more elaborate earlier designs. Scheme A, entitled ''Windsor Castle,'' followed the tradition of the grand ice palaces of the previous century. It would have measured about 300 feet by 205 feet, with a main tower 64 feet high. (Above, front elevation and rear elevation; at right, floor plan)

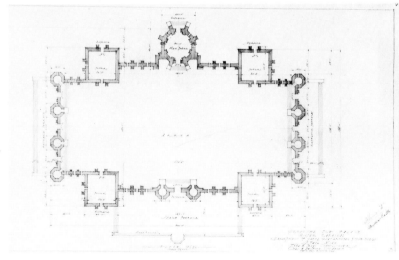

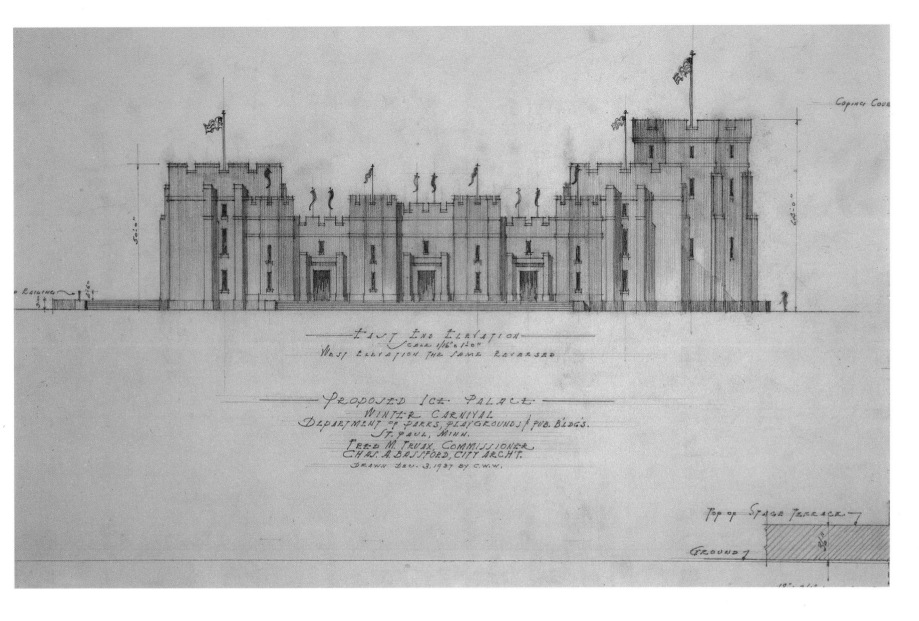

Proposed side elevation for Windsor Castle, St. Paul, 1938.

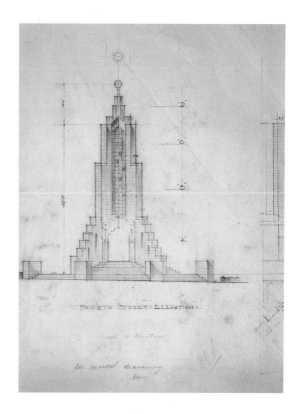

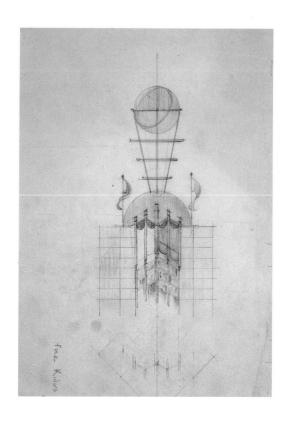

As in Montreal and Québec, in St. Paul the carnival inspired many smaller ice structures. Drawings for the 1940 carnival show this impressive individual tower. Called the Fire King's Throne, capped by a sphere, it overlooked a courtyard.

youths spent three weeks building it, and they used 4,000 tons of ice. At the height of construction, the young workers precariously threaded their way along the tops of the towers in a 35-mile-an-hour gale.

1940

In this "Art Deco" period, St. Paul architects designed single towers, as well as palaces, of ice. Drawings for the 1940 carnival show a majestic individual tower, called the Fire King's Throne, topped by a sphere, overlooking a courtyard. Bassford and Miller prepared these drawings.

The Fire King's Throne probably rose from a 16-foot-square base, buttressed at the corners. Two basic schemes show the tower as either 55 feet or 68 feet high. It was set on an octagonal platform 70 feet in diameter. Eight pylons (4 feet 7 inches square, 6 to 7 feet tall) surrounded the platform. Fourteen larger pylons marked the perimeter of the courtyard. Wabasha, Cedar, Fourth, and Fifth streets bounded the site, which was approximately 315 feet by 280 feet.

Three miles away from the downtown site of the Fire King's Throne lay Como Park, where the 1940 ice palace was built. The WPA granted the ice palace $14,000, which paid for the labor involved. Between forty and sixty builders worked around the clock in three eight-hour shifts for about two weeks.

Bassford and Wigington designed the palace, which was basically a square courtyard, enclosed on three sides. It measured 150 feet by 142 feet. A double throne of ice, 18 feet high, was erected along the open side for the Carnival Queen and King Boreas VI. Behind the throne rose the main tower. Called King's Tower or Tower of the Winds, this tower was 40 feet square in plan and 75 feet in height.

Four other principal towers stood at the corners of the courtyard. The northern tower rose from a circular base 26 feet in diameter to a height of about 30 feet. To the right of the throne

Longest of the modern St. Paul ice palaces, the 1939 palace was a gingerbread fantasy with slits, scallops, and arched entrances. Under NYA auspices, 200 youths spent three weeks building it.

stood the eastern tower. Dubbed "Queen's Tower," it rose from an octagonal base 30 feet in diameter to a height of 40 feet. "Federal Tower" lay to the left of the throne, at the southern corner of the building. A 30-foot cube in form, it housed a post office. Como Tower pinned the western corner. It rose 35 feet from an octagonal base 26 feet in diameter.

The palace rampart was a double wall: two ice walls, each 1 foot 10 inches thick, separated by a 3-foot cavity. The walls of the corner tower were 2 feet 9 inches thick. At King's Tower the wall thickened to 3 feet 8 inches and was supported by buttresses. Four smaller towers, called bastions, were set into the side walls of the building.

1941

Bassford and Wigington designed the ice palace for the 1941 carnival, which resembled that of 1940 in concept. The plan was

City architect Charles Bassford and his assistant, C. W. Wigington, designed many of the modern St. Paul ice castles. Their 1940 scheme was basically a square courtyard, enclosed on three sides. Paid from a WPA grant of $14,000, about 50 builders worked around the clock to construct the castle in two short weeks. At the front of the finished ice palace stood a double throne, ready for the coronation of the Carnival Queen and King Boreas VI. Aluminum-paneled "windows" added extra sparkle.

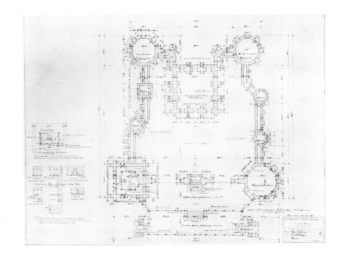

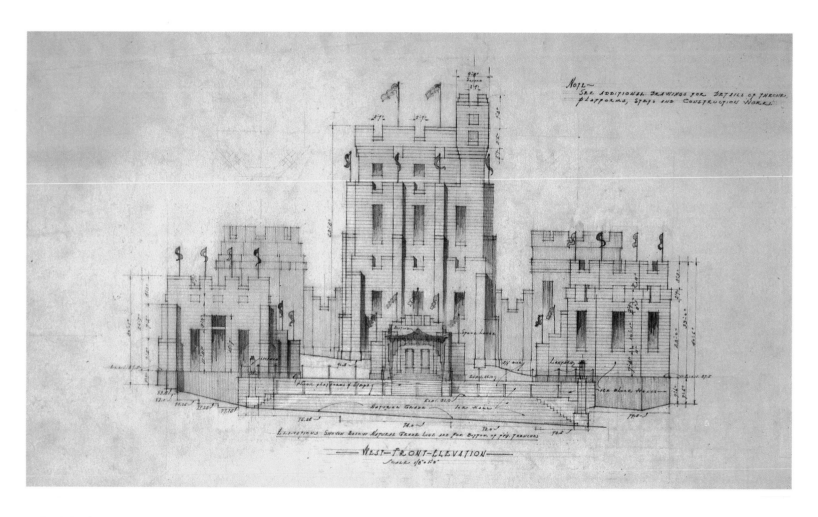

Behind the double throne of the 1940 ice palace, the main tower rose to a height of 75 feet. Four other major towers varied in height from 30 to 40 feet. (Elevation)

This side elevation of the 1940 ice palace shows two of the four small towers, called bastions, which were set into the side walls of the building.

a diamond with one corner cut off; a theatrical throne dominated the open corner. Again the highest tower rose behind the throne.

The art of ice harvesting had not yet died, and ice for the 1941 palace came from McCarron's Lake. The builders used about 22,000 cakes of ice, but, because of breakage, nearly 30,000 had to be supplied. Each block measured 31 inches by 22 inches by 16 inches and weighed 350 pounds.

About 270 men worked on the palace, which was again located in Como Park. The castle measured 123 feet by 123 feet, but it appeared larger. Approaching it from the open corner, one had to notice the 165-foot diagonal axis.

_____

King's Tower, the tallest tower of the 1941 ice palace, rose to a height of approximately 80 feet. In the foreground, long lines of people wait to enter Federal Tower, which housed a special post office. FACING

Workers installed 2,000 bulbs and 3,000 square feet of gelatin color in the space between the ice palace walls. At night, whole wall sections and the round towers periodically changed colors. BELOW

King's Tower, the tallest tower, rose from a 40-foot-square base to a height of approximately 80 feet. At the 60-foot level, the tower became octagonal, with a diameter of about 33 feet. At the western and eastern corners of the palace stood Federal Tower (housing a post office) and Queen's Tower. Each was an octagonal tower, 25 feet in diameter and 30 feet shorter than the main tower. Kabeyun Tower and Wabun Tower flanked the throne. Both were 16 feet square in plan and 40 feet shorter than King's Tower. Two small round turrets flanked King's Tower.

The palace was constructed with ice walls 1 foot 10 inches thick. The space between the walls, a mere cavity in the 1940 palace, grew in this building to a 6 foot 4 inch passageway connecting the towers. This passageway had a practical function. Two thousand bulbs and three thousand square feet of gelatin color were installed there. At night, whole wall sections and the round towers periodically changed colors.

The ice palace walls were thickened to 2 feet 9 inches in Federal Tower, Queen's Tower, Kabeyun Tower, and Wabun

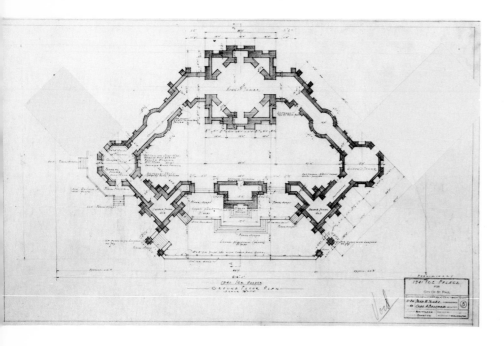

Bassford and Wigington designed the 1941 ice palace, which resembled that of 1940 in concept. Ice walls rose from a diamond-shaped courtyard, open at one corner.

Tower. The mighty King's Tower was supported by 3 foot 8 inch walls. After two weeks of carnival festivities, when a thaw had weakened the ice palace, powerful tractors and a steel cable harness were needed to drag down the "unsafe" towers.

Drawings exist for an earlier scheme for the 1941 ice palace, which included two additional towers. In this version, peaked roofs capped some of the towers.

1942

Bassford and Wigington also designed the 1942 ice palace, which was erected on the Highland Park Golf Course. This palace, the last one built until after World War II, melted because of unseasonable weather. The undaunted St. Paulites staged a storming of the palace remnants. "Green and red rockets, sulphurous fumes and brilliant flares illuminated the doomed structure."[5]

Two side towers flanked a tall central tower. A throne was set up against the main tower, and terraces spread out in front of it. The whole structure measured approximately 170 by 80 feet.

The main tower, King's Tower, rose to a platform at 50 feet high as an octagonal cylinder 40 feet in diameter. A circular cylinder 16 feet high and 14 feet in diameter rested on top of it, bringing the ice to a height of 66 feet in this tower. Four buttresses fanned out around the cylinder, giving it a dome-like appearance. A huge lantern took the tower to a total height of 80 feet.

At the northwest end of the palace stood Federal Tower. It measured 62 feet by 31 feet by 38 feet high. An apse 18 feet in diameter protruded from each end. The post office planned for this tower would have sold defense bonds.

Queen's Tower guarded the southeastern end of the ice palace. Its dimensions are identical to those of Federal Tower, except for its length, which was 42 feet instead of 62 feet.

The walls of King's Tower were 2 feet 9 inches thick; those of the side towers, 1 foot 10 inches thick. Six-foot-wide passageways connected the main tower to the side towers.

1947

Although winter carnivals have been held in St. Paul every year since 1946, only occasionally have ice palaces been built. A small ice palace went up at Fourth Street and Cedar Street in 1949. The 1947 carnival, which introduced the National Outdoor Speed Skating Championships and an ice fishing contest, planned a large ice palace.

R. G. Zelzer and C. W. Wigington designed the structure, which began to rise on the Highland Park Golf Course. The scheme consisted of three towers, connected by a slightly curved passageway. A double throne was set into the tallest tower; a coronation platform extended in front of it.

The palace would have measured approximately 210 feet in

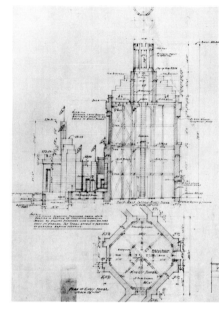

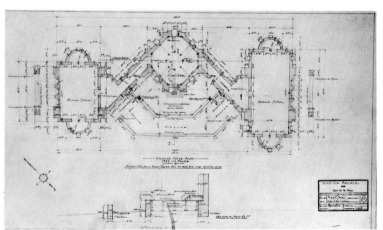

A warm spell melted the 1942 ice palace, the last one attempted until after World War II. The undaunted St. Paulites staged a storming of the palace remnants. King's Tower (the main tower) would have risen to a height of 80 feet, and the post office planned for Federal Tower would have sold defense bonds. These drawings show the front elevation, a section, and the floor plan of the partially built palace. The section (above, right) shows the interior wooden structure that permitted access to all the major towers of this period.

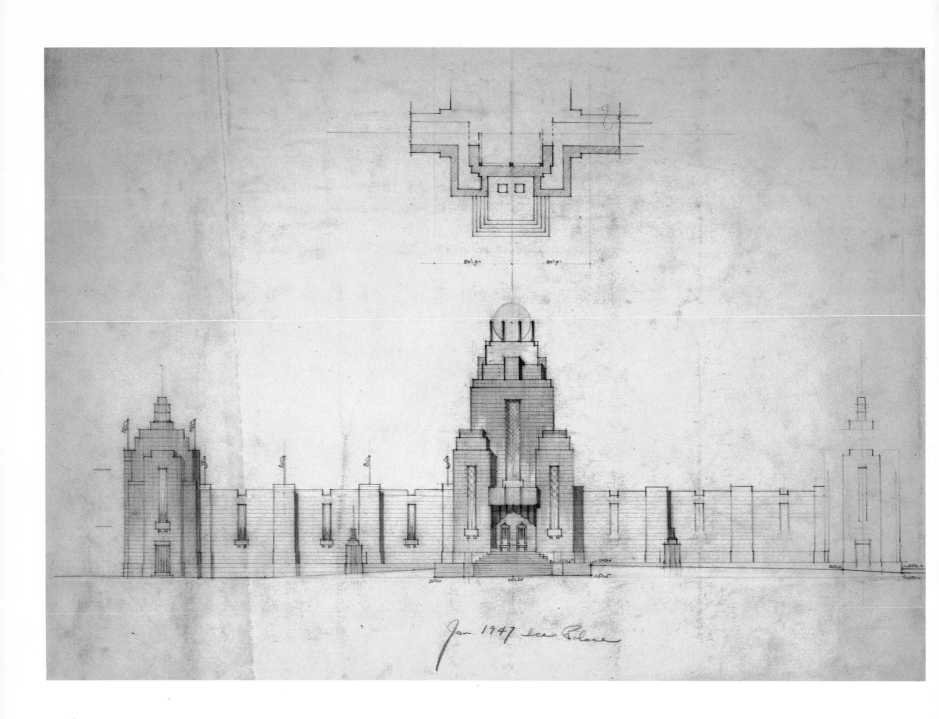

Jan 1947 Ice Palace

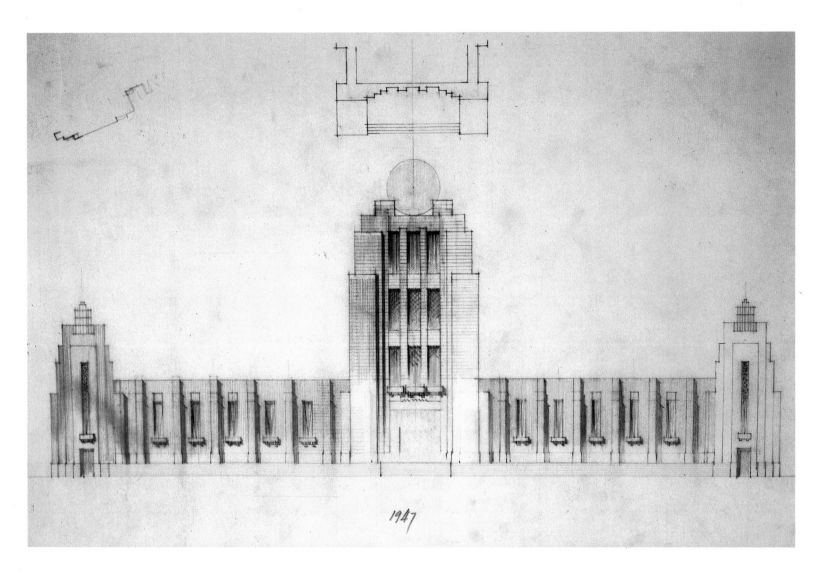

1947

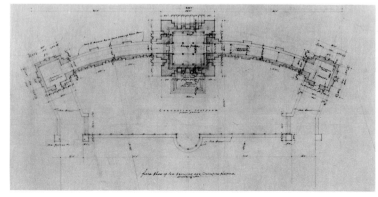

R. G. Zelzer and C. W. Wigington designed the 1947 ice palace, which began to rise on the Highland Park Golf Course. The palace would have measured approximately 210 feet in length and varied considerably in width. The scheme consisted of three towers, connected by a slightly curved passageway. (On page 100, front elevation; above, alternate front elevation; at right, floor plan)

Bob Olsen (today an architect and ice palace historian) initiated, designed, and built this 1975 ice palace. ABOVE

Craig Rafferty and Jeri Zuber designed this ice palace for the American Bicentennial. Images of "turrets," a "maze," and a "great hall" are evoked by bends and changes in height of the nested walls, rather than shaped as discrete medieval elements. (Isometric and perspective drawings) RIGHT, AND FACING

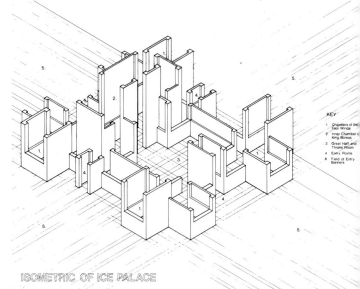

KEY

1 Chambers of the Four Winds
2 Inner Chamber of King Boreas
3 Great Hall and Throne Room
4 Entry Points
5 Field of Entry Banners

ISOMETRIC OF ICE PALACE

length and varied considerably in width. King's Tower (the central tower) rose from a base of 36 feet square, supported by clasping buttresses, to a height of 60 feet of ice. A lantern brought the total height of the tower to 75 feet. At the right end of the palace stood Federal Tower, measuring 20 feet by 20 feet by 40 feet high and housing a post office. Queen's Tower, at the opposite end, had identical dimensions. Cylindrical lanterns topped Federal Tower and Queen's Tower.

A six-foot-wide passageway connected the three towers. The passage walls were 1 foot 10 inches thick and attained a height of about 23 feet. Drawings exist for two basic schemes. One shows the central tower topped by a globular lantern, and the other by one that is cylindrical.

Unfortunately, the palace was never completed. In late January, when construction was about one-third accomplished, warm weather turned the rising walls and towers "into a gooey and hazardous mess."[6] Vulcan stormed the ruins during the carnival, with fireworks and a pass by a P-51 fighter plane.

1975

When plans for the 1975 Winter Carnival were underway, a student from Saint Olaf College, in Northfield, Minnesota, appeared in the carnival manager's office.

"Why don't you build ice palaces for the carnival any more?" asked the student, Robert A. Olsen.

"Why don't you build one for us?" asked the manager, Gene Strommen.

So Bob Olsen (today an architect and ice palace historian) designed and built the 1975 palace.

The art department sponsored the ice palace as an independent study, and Olsen received college credit for his achievement. He headed a crew of about eight workers during the week, and, on weekends, two forklift-type trucks sped a double crew along.

The castle measured 100 feet by 42 feet by 36 feet high. It used 1,400 blocks of manufactured ice, each block measuring 1 foot by 2 feet by 4 feet and weighing 400 pounds. The palace cost $13,900.

1976

For the American Bicentennial, the Minnesota Society of Architects sponsored a competition for an ice palace design. Jeri Zuber and Craig Rafferty submitted the winning proposal.

Their palace rose from an elegant "Minnesota grid," based on the module of the ice block. (Each manufactured block measured 1 foot by 2 feet by 4 feet 6 inches.) The palace as a whole measured approximately 104 feet by 93 feet by 40 feet high.

The floor plan was symmetrical. Clean segments of wall varied dramatically in height, rising to 8 feet, 16 feet, 24 feet, 32 feet, or 40 feet.

The outermost wall bent to form four "turrets," commemorating the four winds of the St. Paul ice palace legend. The space between the outer and inner walls became a "maze," and the inner walls in turn framed a "great hall" and a "tower," 40 feet high.

These images are evoked by bends and changes in height of the nested walls, rather than being shaped as discrete medieval elements. The fact that this palace can be comfortably analyzed as a series of modulated walls makes it spiritual kin to the one of 1937.

8

Snow and Ice: Sapporo and Québec

Sapporo, 1950 to the Present

In 1950, President Harry Truman ordered the development of the hydrogen bomb, and North Korean Communist forces invaded South Korea. In between these two events, some teenagers in Sapporo, Japan, initiated a thriving snow festival. That February and every February since, the people of Sapporo have constructed huge statues of ice and snow, some of which take the form of buildings.

Sapporo is the capital of Hokkaido, the northernmost of Japan's four main islands. Hokkaido has its own aboriginal people, the Ainu, a relatively sparse population, and a strong fishing industry. The island has forty volcanoes, in various stages of activity. Japanese lords established fiefs in southern Hokkaido in the fifteenth century, but the Japanese did not settle the island in large numbers until four centuries later, at the urging of the national government. Hokkaido's five months of daily snow may have discouraged earlier immigrants.

Sapporo presents a clean, modern appearance. American engineers, invited to help spur its development, laid out wide, tree-lined streets in 1871. Sapporo partakes of Hokkaido's bitter winter. According to one observer, the "sidewalks are so packed with plowed snow that they stand four feet above the ground, and its citizens think nothing of beginning each day by digging out from the drifts accumulated the night before."[1] Sapporo, however, has turned its climate into an attraction. In addition to

Sapporo, capital of Hokkaido, hosts the most famous snow festival on the island. High school students originated the idea and built the statues for the first festival in 1950. This ice palace was built in 1975.
LEFT

Hawaiian King Kamehameha sees snow for the first time, as he stands in front of Iolani Palace, complete with frozen palm trees. (Sapporo, 1982) FACING

holding the Snow Festival every year, the city gained worldwide recognition when it hosted the Winter Olympics in 1972.

Winter holidays focusing on children have a traditional basis in Japan. In Yokote, in northern Honshu (Japan's main island), an older festival takes place. The children build "kamakura," houses of snow, every February. Inside these little hemispherical dwellings, they enshrine the God of Water and hold cozy parties.

The First Sapporo Snow Festival was organized in 1950 by civic leaders and six high schools. Fifty thousand visitors came to see seven ice sculptures created by students from the schools. In 1968, crowds totaling 3,900,000 people viewed 150 sculptures. Although the Sapporo Festival is for adults as well as for children, slides are carved into some of the statues especially for the smaller visitors.

Frozen works of art appear in two main sites—Odori Park and Makomanai Military Base. The former is a generous ribbon of greenery (in summer) dividing the city's main thoroughfare; the latter lies at the city's outskirts. Odori is a distinctively urban site; at night bold neon lights bounce off the statues. Makomanai is quieter and less crowded. The International Snow Sculpture Competition, started in 1973, takes place in the square in front of the city hall.

Other festival activities include jingling horse-drawn sleigh rides and a contest for Snow Queen. Entertainers in colorful kimonos perform traditional Japanese dances, and hardy Sapporo musicians play popular music on an outdoor organ. There are skating rinks in the city and skiing areas nearby.

For the 33rd Snow Festival, in 1982, trucks carted in almost 5,000 loads of snow for the statues. Thirteen giant sculptures went up, of which ten were snow and three were ice. The total number of statues reached 190. Ten countries competed in the

International Sculpture Competition, with mainland China and Sweden attending for the first time.

Young people are no longer the only sculptors. At the Citizens' Square, groups of citizens from every walk of life make snow statues. Hachiro Takahashi, who creates Kabuki figures as tall as 43 feet, starts working on them fifteen days before the holiday. Since 1955, members of the army have sculpted giant figures and buildings. There were ten of these at the 26th Snow Festival; the largest one measured 46 feet by 92 feet by 79 feet high.

Giant snow statues require special technology. Nowadays the planners draw up a blueprint and make a miniature model. The soldiers build a plywood frame, inside a frame of logs and boards. They use vehicles called snow flushers to pack snow into the frames. The statues face north to minimize melting of details. The builders pack in snow from the southern side of the structure, increasing the density of snow on the main, northern facade. Snow packed this way turns into a solid mass in a few days.

Soldiers from Makomanai spent nineteen days building an image of the Buddhist god of love for the 19th Snow Festival (1968). They used 220 truckloads of snow.

Within a wood frame they first packed a 62-foot-square, three-foot-high platform of snow. Into this they anchored wood shafts to support the torso and head. Then, tier by tier, day by day, they constructed a huge layer cake of ice around the supports. Heavy-booted squads stomped each successive layer into its temporary frame and doused it with water to freeze in overnight temperatures of 15 degrees to 25 degrees F. Again and again they repeated the process until the basic shape emerged, a stepped pyramid that towered 33 feet.[2]

Once the frozen mass is ready, cutting begins. Tools used range from the heavy to the small, and even include soup bowls. The workers wear special clothing to protect them from the cold. In 1968, the soldiers working on the god of love first hacked out his rough contours. "To fashion his six arms, they molded water-softened ice around wood cores wrapped in straw. Finally, hatchet-

This building of ice was constructed in 1981, as part of the 32nd Sapporo Snow Festival.

The Japanese Cooks' Association built this ice building. It reproduces the Vasily Blazhenny Cathedral in Moscow. (Sapporo, 1978) ABOVE

This giant snow complex, called Munich Square, was erected by Japanese soldiers in 1977. FACING

and-chisel-wielding sculptors fashioned the fine details of the enormous figure. Their model was a 700-year-old wood carving of the god only a foot tall.[3]

Finishing touches include the removal of any pebbles or hardened mud, which absorb heat and melt the snow. In the "make up" stage, pure white snow is mixed with water and patted on the statue by hand. This thick sherbet-like mixture freezes into a skin which both beautifies and protects the creation. (Ice, you may remember from Chapter 2, is impermeable and stronger than snow.)

Sapporo's architectural constructions are statues rather than true buildings. Unlike Western ice palaces, they lack interiors and cannot be entered. These Japanese palaces of ice and snow must be admired, however, for their exquisite detail. Images sculpted have included: a "dream castle of ice," a replica of the first Japanese government headquarters in Hokkaido, a model of the Hokkaido Centennial Memorial Tower, a castle backdrop for Snow White and the Seven Dwarfs, a copy of Phoenix Hall in Kyoto City, Cinderella's palace, and Osaka Castle.

One structure that did have an interior was built in Chitose, Hokkaido, in 1982. (In recent years, snow festivals have sprung up all over the island.) Chitose is located near Lake Shikotsuko, a popular summer resort:

By the time we arrived, a soft mist had enveloped the lake and trees, shrouding the distant mountains in white. It was an eerily beautiful scene and suited Lake Shikotsuko's version of the snow festival perfectly. The imaginative sculptors there had created a Gothic festival of ice caves lit by spotlights of green and pink. The sculptors first constructed a wooden frame and then poured water over it. The water froze in drips to create a ghostly cave with icicles hanging down from its arched roof. Some mischievous craftsmen constructed a maze of ice and a tough,

slippery climb up a hill through a cave. Finally, of course, was a slide for the children.[4]

To prevent accidents, all constructions are destroyed at the end of the festivals. Eiji Miyazawa comments: ". . . Japanese art, poetry, and philosophy have always dwelt on the impermanence and fleeting nature of all things, whether cherry blossoms, snowflakes, ice sculptures—or human life itself."[5]

Québec, 1955 to the Present

In 1955, West Germany became a sovereign state, and Argentina ousted Juan Perón. In the United States, President Eisenhower suffered a coronary thrombosis, and Martin Luther King, Jr., led a successful boycott of an Alabama bus system. In Canada, Louis S. St. Laurent was prime minister, and a group of Québec businessmen founded the modern Québec Winter Carnival.

The Carnival de Québec has become a magnet for tourists. Thousands of visitors come to enjoy the sports, the enthusiasm of the natives, and the excellent Québec food. Every year, a palace of ice or snow is built on a portion of the old city wall, in the Place Carnaval.

The "Bonhomme Carnaval," a jovial snowman, symbolizes the affair. He appears in many guises, on street decorations and on souvenirs. In his most mobile form, played by an actor in a white suit, he attends carnival functions and imprisons (for about ten minutes) offenders who neglect to smile. In a 1962 interview, Noel Moisan explained that he had to keep himself in "perfect" physical condition in order to move lightly as Bonhomme Carnaval, since the snowman's foam rubber and synthetic fur costume weighed fifty-four pounds.

Seven sections of Québec each select a beautiful young woman as a duchess for the festive pre-Lenten period. Bonhomme Carnaval crowns one of them as Carnival Queen, at the ice palace.

". . . Japanese art, poetry, and philosophy have always dwelt on the impermanence and fleeting nature of all things, whether cherry blossoms, snowflakes, ice sculptures—or human life itself." FACING

1962

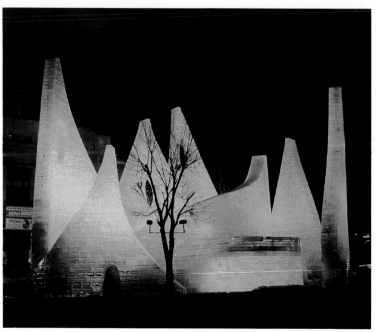

1965

A group of Québec businessmen founded the Carnaval de Qŭebec in 1955. Every year, thousands of visitors come to enjoy the sports, the enthusiasm of the natives, and the excellent food. Ice palaces like these, sculptural and abstract in style, were designed by local architects.

A tremendous number of activities goes on. Traditional ones such as the canoe race, broomball, and tobogganing have continued. Nowadays, the night parade features motorized floats lit by electric lights, instead of snowshoers carrying torches. Innovations include races, on ice or snow, for motorcycles, cars, and snowmobiles; Pee-wee Hockey, for ten- to twelve-year-old athletes; and the international snow sculpture contest, in which teams of rugged competitors carve large works of art. Some of the sculptors glaze their creations with water to give them an icy patina.

The ice palaces built for this ongoing carnival vary considerably in form. Those that appear quite modern and abstract were always designed by architects, although architects also designed some of the medieval-style ice castles.

In 1955, the first year of the modern Carnaval de Québec, a committee of architects, engineers, and contractors was responsible for the ice palace. Prominent members included Roland Dupéré, an architect, and Roger Desjardins, an engineer. Jean-Baptiste Soucy, director of l'Ecole des Beaux-Arts de Québec, drew up the actual plans. The palace included two unusual "futuriste" towers, one of which was built by some Ecole des Beaux-Arts students. A crowd of over 15,000 flocked to the palace opening.

J.-B. Soucy also designed the ice palace of 1956. Raoul Hunter made the pressed paper statue of Bonhomme Carnaval that stood in front of it.

Germain Chabot, a Québec architect, designed an ice palace and fort for the 1957 carnival.

In 1962, the high spirits following the carnival opening

erupted into a fist fight and smashed windows, and five young men were sent to jail. The ice palace committee that year included André Robitaille, an architect, and Paul A. Emond, a contractor. A crew of about eleven men built the castle in seventeen days. Using 400 tons of ice and standing 65 feet high, the palace was the biggest since the start of the carnival eight years earlier.

The contractor Emond also served on the ice palace committee for 1965, along with the architect Paul Gauthier. Emond constructed many Québec ice palaces, including those of 1972, 1977, and 1978.

The first eleven ice palaces had been erected in Place d'Youville, but that of 1966 went up in Place d'Armes. The workmen constructed it around the Monument de la Foi, which they protected with a wooden structure. Circumstances beyond their control caused extensive revisions in the castle plans, but the finished castle, 60 feet high, was eminently satisfactory. The builders used about 4,000 blocks of ice, which weighed 400 pounds each.

Since 1967, Gaston Robert has designed most of the castles in a medieval mode. Robert, a former window dresser and an accomplished float designer, runs the carnival corporation.

In 1967, Place d'Youville was restored as the palace site. For the first time, the castle included plywood as well as ice. At its inauguration, the lieutenant governor, the Carnival Queen, and Bonhomme Carnaval put their fingers together on a button that instantaneously lit up the whole building.

The palace of 1968 measured 196 feet by 34 feet by 60 feet high, used fiberglass towers, and cost $17,000.

Princess Grace of Monaco thrilled the people of Québec by attending the 1969 Carnival. The idea for that year's ice palace came from a draftsman in the Roads Department. The castle measured 115 feet by 40 feet by 53 feet high. It contained a dungeon, and was adorned by a giant crown. Consisting of 2,500 blocks of ice, weighing 400 pounds each, the castle cost about $22,000.

The 1970 palace had eleven towers. It measured approxi-

Gaston Robert designed this composite palace of ice, plywood, and fiberglass in 1967. Robert, a former window dresser and an accomplished float designer, runs the carnival corporation.

mately 104 feet by 20 feet by 50 feet high. A construction team erected it in twenty-four days, and 61,500 watts of electricity made it gleam at night.

In 1971, the ice castle used 1,200 blocks of ice.

The ice palace of 1972 cost $20,000. It measured 80 feet by 23 feet by 54 feet high. Fifteen workmen assembled it from about 1,300 blocks of ice.

The lovely palace of 1974 ran into problems. Mild weather,

This handsome ice palace, built in 1966 from 4,000 blocks of ice, combines both modern and medieval elements. The main tower rose 60 feet. FACING

This ice palace marked the twentieth Carnaval de Québec in 1974. Damaged by warm weather but skillfully repaired, the castle cost $50,000. Increasing construction costs led the carnival committee to switch to snow palaces in 1979. ABOVE

sun, and rain caused various damage. Four of the giant stalagmites collapsed; a fifth leaned so much that it had to be rebuilt. In the end, however, the repairs were accomplished so skillfully that no one could complain. The castle used about 4,000 blocks of ice and cost $50,000.

In 1975, architects Belzile, Brassard and Gallienne designed the palace. It incorporated 3,000 blocks of ice and stood 35 feet tall.

The castle of 1976 measured approximately 165 feet by 50 feet by 60 feet high.

The 1977 ice palace measured 139 feet by 51 feet by 56 feet high. The builders used fiberglass as well as ice for this $80,000 building.

Paul Emond brought in the 1978 ice palace for $47,000. It measured 150 feet by 52 feet by 50 feet high.

At about this time, the carnival corporation decided that building with ice had become too expensive. From 1979 on, all the Quebec palaces have been built of snow. No longer, alas, do they possess the very special transparency, solidity, and sheen of block ice.

The castle of 1979 was carved from a single huge mass of packed snow. World-renowned snow sculptor Raymond St. Laurent headed the construction team.

Later palaces have been built by a construction method similar to that commonly used for concrete. This process takes about three weeks. While formwork is set up on the palace site, trucks carry in ten-ton loads of virgin snow from the countryside. About 400 loads are required. Work crews pack the snow densely into the formwork. Then the formwork is taken down, leaving a building of pressed snow. Finally, the workmen trace the outlines of imaginary blocks on the palace.

9

State
of the Art

Knowledge about ice and snow construction has advanced tremendously in the twentieth century, largely due to research by the military. In this chapter we shall review contemporary ice palace building techniques, highlight the development of new construction knowledge, and consider some of the ways in which this new knowledge can be applied to future ice palaces.

Modern Ice Palaces

Many twentieth-century ice palaces have been built with masonry techniques quite similar to those used in the nineteenth century. Nowadays, in place of horses, engines power the equipment. In the thirties and forties, in St. Paul, steam cranes hoisted ice

Modern night parades feature motorized floats lit by electric lights, instead of snowshoers carrying torches. (Sapporo, 1981)

blocks as heavy as 800 pounds to the top of the palace walls; giant ice tongs dragged these blocks into position; and wire mesh tied every fourth row together. The workers wore special creepers, so that they would not slip and repeat the tragedy of Ernst Hoempel. By the fifties, in Québec, manufactured ice had replaced cut ice. All the modern St. Paul ice palaces and those built in Québec from 1955 to 1978 were masonry structures, assembled from blocks of ice.

One new technique that has evolved, inspired by twentieth-century concrete construction methods, is the use of cast snow. The builders pack snow into forms, which are later removed. The Québec castles of 1980 and later were built in this way. So far, cast snow buildings have been medieval in style, in contrast to the modernity of their construction method. Their builders have even scored them to look as if they were built from blocks.

The Japanese have invented their own methods of producing architectural sculptures in both snow and ice. They use mounds of snow, blocks of ice, and a great deal of intricate carving. In some cases, armatures of another material provide hidden support for elaborate snow statues.

The Bergship

Early in 1942, warm weather had melted a beautiful ice palace in St. Paul, discouraging ice palace building for several years. Later in 1942, research into ice construction received a boost in a way that no one would have predicted. Geoffrey Pyke, an Englishman, submitted a proposal to the Allied forces that giant aircraft carriers be constructed out of icebergs.

The plan was appealing for a number of reasons: larger carriers would allow the use of faster and better-armed planes; massive air support would be needed if Japan were to be invaded; even an artificial iceberg presumably would be cheaper than metal or wood, which were in short supply; and an airbase of ice never could be sunk. Winston Churchill gave research on the "Bergship" the highest priority.

Ice was systematically and intensively studied for the first time. Naval engineers decided that natural icebergs were too small; they envisioned a huge floating beam of manufactured ice, 2,000 feet long. (Two thousand feet was the minimum length of runway required for bombers at that time.) Artificial refrigeration would help keep the ice at a constant low temperature.

The main problem the engineers discovered was that ice was unreliable as a structural material—particularly when bombarded by explosives! The average ice beam was strong enough to use, but individual beams sometimes ruptured under relatively low stresses. The scientists solved this problem by reinforcing the ice with woodpulp. Ice frozen from water mixed with a small percentage of woodpulp is stronger and much less erratic than ordinary ice.

As the design progressed, the engineers puzzled over other questions. What could they use for the giant rudder? Could the hollow interior of the Bergship be compartmentalized? Where could they build a plant large enough to turn out millions of tons of reinforced ice? They probably could have solved these problems eventually, but new developments made the whole project obsolete: the range of aircraft increased so much that it became possible to cover most of the Atlantic from existing land bases, and the Americans captured enough islands in the Pacific to support the eventual invasion of Japan. Early in 1944, the Bergship was abandoned.

Frozen Frontiers

In the 1950s, international research in Antarctica and military activity in Greenland stimulated wide interest in the properties of snow. Snow is the only easily obtainable material in these areas. As scientists and soldiers penetrated the Arctic regions, our knowledge of snow as a building material was advanced by actual construction.

Arctic conditions make snow excavation an extremely advantageous technique. The lower levels of a snowfield are stronger and more stable than surface snow. They have been compressed by the weight of the snow above them and they have had time to grow stronger through a natural process called sintering. Other benefits of excavation are that temperatures are more even underground and that a buried installation minimizes the formation of snowdrifts.

As early as 1949, a French expedition built a small research base below the surface of the Greenland ice cap. When the U.S. Army decided to build a large nuclear-powered camp on the ice cap in northern Greenland, they adopted an "undersnow" plan. Camp Century, built in 1959 and 1960, spread over an area

In the twentieth century, research by the military has tremendously increased our knowledge of the potential uses for ice and snow as building materials. Here, a cast snow arch roofs an underground army installation. (Camp Century, Greenland, about 1960)

about 1,400 by 1,000 feet. Prefabricated buildings were erected in trenches that lay roughly 25 feet below surface level. (Since about 4 feet of snow fall each year in this area, after five years the floor level was about 45 feet below the surface.)

Another method of using snow explored in Camp Century was casting. Observers had noted that "snow cleared from roads by rotary plows gained significantly in density, hardness, and bearing strength as a result of having been handled by these plows."[1] Therefore the army began to process snow with a rotary plow before applying it to a form. They roofed at least part of Camp Century by covering the trenches with arched metal forms, backfilling over the forms with plowed snow, and removing the forms when the snow had age-hardened.

The U.S. Army has used cast snow to build walls, beams, abutments, columns, and domes, as well as arches. For example, they constructed domes 16 feet to 36 feet in diameter by casting plowed snow over two kinds of forms: inflatable hemispheres (like the bubbles over tennis courts) and sheeted geodesic frames. After the snow had hardened for twelve hours, they removed the forms. The remaining snow domes stood securely on their own.

In all of these projects, snow served as both site and material. One fascinating effort using conventional materials on a snow site should be mentioned—building on stilts. Buildings on the surface of Arctic snowfields tend to attract huge snowdrifts, with one exception. If the structure is elevated 10 to 20 feet above the surface, rapid burial is avoided. Therefore the U.S. Army has built certain buildings on expandable columns, powered by hydraulic jacks, which permit annual lifting and leveling. Of course this is an extremely expensive method of construction. It

has been used only for such facilities as aircraft control and missile warning installations, which must be built above the surface.

One last technique that U.S. military engineers have studied is snow compaction. In the great forests of the northern hemisphere, loggers compacted snow roads with drags or wooden rollers. They noticed that these methods worked only on shallow snow. To "produce a compacted layer thick enough to support traffic on deep snow," they introduced the first "depth processors."[2]

They used a harrow set with prongs extending into the snow, an open roller, and a roller with swinging flails. These devices produced a thicker supporting layer because they mixed the snow, to a considerable depth, as they compacted it. Mixing the snow leads to age-hardening, just as plowing the snow with a rotary snow plow does.

During World War II, a Russian named Kragelski developed a depth-processing method of compaction effective on snow up to 24 inches deep. Following his concept, the U.S. Navy developed power-driven mixers. They have used these snow mixers to build such feats as: a 33-inch-thick aircraft runway, a parking lot that held 11,000 cars, and a four-mile road, all composed entirely of ice and snow.

Thin Shells of Ice

Knowledge about ice has expanded rapidly, even in the short stretch of time since the Bergship project. The Bergship engineers erred in thinking that unreliability was the major problem in building with ice. Ice is a very complex material, and early methods of testing produced unreliable data. The major problem in ice construction, aside from melting, is creep.

Creep is the slow deformation of a structure over a long period of time. Ice is much stronger when loaded rapidly than when loaded slowly. (Materials are tested by adding weight to them.) To visualize creep, assume an aircraft landing on an ice field. During the impact of landing, the ice does not fail. If the

The future of ice palaces may hold large-span, thin shell structures. The design of such ice shells could be inspired by Byzantine architecture or by the most modern construction. The work of Frei Otto, shown here, could be translated beautifully into ice.

Thin shells are an appropriate form for ice because their lightness and efficiency minimize creep. These structures also can be very beautiful. Shell structures developed by man and nature include domes, barrel vaults, hyperbolic paraboloids, and conoids.

Our knowledge of frozen shell structures comes from only a couple of sources. Wolf Hilberts (an architect who is presently exploring new technology for underwater structures) has erected small ice shells in Fargo, North Dakota. Fred Anderes and Dr. Frederick Roll of the University of Pennsylvania have performed careful scientific analysis on a miniature ice dome (30 inches in

plane remains there for days, however, it slowly sinks into the ice.

We became interested in the nature of ice in the hope that we could design cheaper but equally beautiful ice palaces. Construction costs of all kinds have soared in the twentieth century, and ice is no exception. Increasing prices drove the Carnaval de Québec to turn from ice to snow.

One promising new method of using ice is in thin shell structures. Any structure that supports itself with a very thin layer of material is a shell; an egg shell is a good example. Only with twentieth-century mathematics have engineers been able to analyze shell structures and stretch buildings to their largest, thinnest, and most efficient forms.

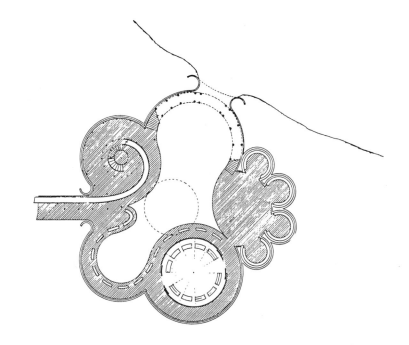

Fred Anderes designed this thin shell ice palace to overlook a lake on Mount Mansfield, Vermont. A complex of domes opens onto the frozen lake, allowing skaters to glide back and forth between the palace and open skies. (At left, interior of plaster model. Below, plan and section) FACING

Perhaps, if ice palace enthusiasts and future ice palace enthusiasts voice their desires, a renaissance of these wonderful structures will flower. Then each of us will have the opportunity to wander through the crystal halls of a shimmering building of ice. RIGHT

THE DEWA

diameter and one-quarter inch thick) to see if much larger domes can be built. The dome was constructed by spraying an inflated balloon with water in a cold chamber. It held 750 pounds (about 125 pounds per square inch) before it collapsed, and its creep was relatively small.

These experiments indicate that large-span thin ice shells will support their own weight, resist wind and other loads, and deform much less than other ice buildings. To build such ice shells, inflatable structures could be used as formwork and later removed. Beautiful translucent shells of ice would be left. Their design could be reminiscent of Byzantine architecture or the work of Frei Otto. Such thin shell ice palaces could be used in winter carnivals and also in ski areas.

To understand the possible sizes of thin shell ice structures, let us concentrate on domes, which are easy to visualize. Using ordinary ice, domes 75 to 100 feet in diameter easily could be constructed. Reinforcement in the ice, such as paper fibers or sawdust, would make domes 300 feet or larger possible.

Fred Anderes has worked out one possible design for a thin shell ice palace. Poised on top of Mount Mansfield, Vermont, next to a lake, the project centers on a dome, 80 feet in diameter, with a round opening on top. This main dome is buttressed by apsidal domes, 20 to 60 feet in diameter. The structural reasoning parallels that of the famous Hagia Sophia in Istanbul.

Skiers enter the project by foot or toboggan from a summit house (where they leave their skis). Inside the palace, they find a skating rink, a stage, and a heated dome. The structure opens out onto the lake, allowing skaters to glide back and forth between the glassy dome and open skies.

The Future of Ice Palaces

Now that you almost have finished this book, we hope that you, like us, have become confirmed ice palace lovers. The great age of ice palace building is, alas, over. No true ice palaces (as opposed to palaces of snow and sculptures of ice) have been built since 1978. But, if ice palace enthusiasts all over the world voice their desires, perhaps a renaissance will flower. Old methods of building can be revived or new ones, like those discussed in this chapter, can be tried out. Then each of us can have the opportunity, which we have only imagined, of wandering through a vast, translucent structure of graceful form and shifting color—a magical building of ice.

Notes

INTRODUCTION

1. *The Northwest Illustrated Monthly Magazine*, vol. VI, No. 2 (February 1888), p. 4.
2. Edgar Andrew Collard, "Of Many Things . . . Palaces of Ice," *The Gazette*, Montreal (December 10, 1977).
3. St. Paul Winter Carnival Association, "The Crystal Carnival" (1886), p. 2.
4. *Northwest Illustrated Monthly*, p. 4.
5. Robert Arthur Olsen, "A History of the Saint Paul Ice Palaces," p. 2.
6. *Northwest Illustrated Monthly*, p. 5.
7. *Ibid.*, p. 1.
8. "The Crystal Carnival," p. 2.
9. Olsen, p. 4.
10. "St. Paul's First Winter Carnival," *Brick Pomeroy's Democrat* (1886), p. 5.

CHAPTER 1

1. George Wolffgang Krafft, *Description et Représentation Exacte de la Maison de Glace, construite à St. Petersbourg au mois de Janvier 1740*, translated from the German by Pierre Louis LeRoy, St. Petersburg, 1741, p. 9.
2. *Horizon* Magazine editors, *The Horizon History of Russia*, 1970, p. 190.
3. Mina Curtiss, *A Forgotten Empress*, New York, p. 256.
4. *Ibid.*, p. 257.
5. *Ibid.*, p. 258.
6. Krafft, p. 8.
7. Curtiss, p. 268.
8. *Ibid.*, p. 261.
9. *Ibid.*, p. 262.
10. *Ibid.*
11. *Ibid.*

CHAPTER 2

1. *St. Paul Pioneer Press*, January 12, 1896.
2. St. Paul Winter Carnival Association, "St. Paul Ice Palace Illustrated," 1886–1887, p. 3.
3. *Ibid.*, p. 3.
4. *Ibid.*, p. 3.
5. *St. Paul Pioneer Press.*
6. St. Paul Winter Carnival Association, p. 3.
7. *Ibid.*
8. *St. Paul Dispatch*, January 4, 1888.

CHAPTER 3

1. Edgar Andrew Collard, "Of Many Things . . . Palaces of Ice," *The Gazette*, Montreal, December 10, 1977.
2. *The New York Times*, January 27, 1885. © 1885 by The New York Times Company. Reprinted by permission.
3. Julian Ralph, *Montreal Star*, 1887 Carnival Number.
4. *Montreal Star*, 1884 Carnival Number.
5. Collard, "Of Many Things . . ."
6. *Montreal Star*, 1884 Carnival Number.
7. January 27, 1885. © 1885 by The New York Times Company. Reprinted by permission.
8. Samuel Edward Dawson, *Mon-*

treal Winter Carnival, 1884, Supplement to *Dawson's Handbook* for the City of Montreal, p. 5.

9. *Ibid.*, p. 16.
10. *Ibid.*, p. 9.
11. Collard, "Of Many Things . . ."
12. *Montreal Star*, 1884 Carnival Number.
13. *The New York Times*, January 27, 1885. © 1885 by The New York Times Company. Reprinted by permission.
14. *Montreal Witness*, 1885 Carnival Number, p. 3.
15. *Ibid.*, p. 11.
16. January 27, 1885. © 1885 by The New York Times Company. Reprinted by permission.
17. *The New York Times*, January 28, 1885. © 1885 by The New York Times Company. Reprinted by permission.
18. *Ibid.*, February 7, 1887. © 1887 by The New York Times Company. Reprinted by permission.
19. *Ibid.* © 1887 by The New York Times Company. Reprinted by permission.
20. *Montreal Witness*, 1887 Carnival Number.
21. Edwin Wildman, "The Passing of the Ice Carnival," *Outing*, January 1899, p. 363.
22. *Montreal Star*, 1887 Carnival Number.
23. *The New York Times*, February 10, 1887. © 1887 by The New York Times Company. Reprinted by permission.
24. Ralph, *Montreal Star*.
25. February 9, 1889.
26. *Ibid.*
27. *Canadian Pictorial*, January 14, 1909, p. 1
28. *Montreal Witness*, February 11, 1909.
29. *The Gazette*, Montreal, February 12, 1909.
30. *Ibid.*, February 20, 1909.
31. *Montreal Witness*, January 14,

1910.
32. *The Gazette*, Montreal, February 4, 1910.

CHAPTER 4

1. St. Paul Winter Carnival Association, "Saint Paul Winter Carnival Souvenir Booklet, 1886–1961."
2. St. Paul Winter Carnival Association, "St. Paul Ice Palace Illustrated," 1886–1887, p. 2.
3. "St. Paul Ice Palace Illustrated," p. 2.
4. "St. Paul Winter Carnival Souvenir Booklet."
5. St. Paul Winter Carnival Association, "The Crystal Carnival," 1886, p. 2.
6. *Ibid.*, p. 6.
7. *The Northwest Illustrated Monthly Magazine*, vol. VI, No. 2 (February 1888), p. 5.
8. "The Crystal Carnival," p. 4.
9. *Ibid.*
10. "St. Paul Ice Palace Illustrated," p. 2.
11. "St. Paul's First Winter Carnival," *Brick Pomeroy's Democrat*, 1886, p. 5.
12. *Ibid.*
13. *Ibid.*
14. *Ibid.*
15. February 7, 1888.
16. January 26, 1888.
17. St. Paul Winter Carnival Association, "History, St. Paul Winter Carnival," p. 3.
18. *St. Paul Pioneer Press*, January 25, 1942.
19. *Ibid.*, January 22, 1896.
20. St. Paul Winter Carnival Association, "St. Paul Winter Carnival," 1896, inside back cover.

CHAPTER 5

1. *The 1973 World Almanac and Book of Facts*, p. 534.
2. J.-T. Coulombe, "Carnavals

d'autrefois," p. 2.
3. *The Gazette*, Montreal, January 30, 1894.
4. *Ibid.*, January 31, 1894.
5. *Daily Mercury*, Québec, January 31, 1894.
6. *Ibid.*
7. *The Gazette*, Montreal, February 3, 1894.
8. *Ibid.*
9. *Ibid.*, January 27, 1896.
10. *Ibid.*
11. *Daily Mercury*, Québec, January 27, 1896.
12. *The Gazette*, Montreal, January 31, 1896.
13. *Ibid.*, February 1, 1896.
14. *The New York Times*, January 18, 1895. © 1895 by The New York Times Company. Reprinted by permission.
15. *The Ottawa Journal*, January 9, 1895.
16. January 23, 1895.
17. January 28, 1895.
18. *The Burlington Free Press and Times*, January 28, 1895.
19. *The Ottawa Citizen*, February 4, 1904.
20. *Ibid.*
21. *The Ottawa Citizen*, January 24, 1922.
22. *Ibid.*, January 31, 1922.
23. *Ibid.*, January 30, 1922.
24. *Ibid.*, January 18, 1922.
25. *The Ottawa Journal*, February 4, 1922.
26. *The Ottawa Citizen*, February 4, 1922.

CHAPTER 6

1. John J. Lipsey, "When Leadville Built a Palace of Ice," *Week End*, March 1, 1957.
2. Edward Blair, "Palace of Ice," Leadville, Colorado, 1977, p. 35.
3. *Ibid.*, p. 37.
4. Mrs. James R. Harvey, "The Leadville Ice Palace of 1896," *Colorado Magazine* (May

1940), p. 95.
5. Blair, p. 24.
6. The Leadville Crystal Carnival Association, "Leadville Crystal Carnival," Leadville, Colorado, January 1896, p. 19.
7. D. Longwell, "The Leadville Ice Palace," May 15, 1968, p. 3.

CHAPTER 7

1. *St. Paul Pioneer Press*, February 2, 1937.
2. *Ibid.*, January 25, 1937.
3. *Ibid.*, February 7, 1937.
4. *Ibid.*, January 28, 1940, p. 3.
5. *Ibid.*, February 2, 1942, p. 6.
6. Robert Arthur Olsen, "A History of the Saint Paul Ice Palaces," p. 50.

CHAPTER 8

1. Susan Chira, "Where Japan Celebrates Winter," *The New York Times*, Sunday, January 16, 1983, Travel Section, p. 14. © 1983 by The New York Times Company. Reprinted by permission.
2. Eiji Miyazawa, (Black Star), "Snow Festival in Japan's Far North," *National Geographic*, Vol. 134, No. 6 (December 1968), p. 826.
3. *Ibid.*
4. Chira, p. 36. © 1983 by The New York Times Company. Reprinted by permission.
5. Miyazawa, p. 832.

CHAPTER 9

1. Elmer F. Clark, "Camp Century" (CRREL TR 174), p. 8.
2. Albert F. Wuori, "Snow Stabilization Studies," *Ice and Snow*, edited by W. D. Kingery, p. 439.

Bibliography

Anderes, Fred, and Dr. Frederick Roll. "Creep and Ultimate Strength of a Thin Shell Ice Dome."

Blair, Edward. "Palace of Ice." Timberline Books, Ltd., Leadville, Colorado, 1977.

The Burlington Free Press and Times, (February 7, 1888; February 9, 1889; January 28, 1895).

Canadian Pictorial. January 14, 1909, p. 1.

Chira, Susan. "Where Japan Celebrates Winter." *The New York Times*, Sunday, January 16, 1983, Travel Section, pp. 14 and 36.

Collard, Edgar Andrew. "Of Many Things . . . Palaces of Ice." *The Gazette*, Montreal, December 10, 1977.

Coquoz, Rene L. "King Pleasure Reigned in 1896." Johnson Publishing Company, Boulder, Colorado, 1973.

Coulombe, J.-T. "Carnavals d'autrefois." Archives de la Ville de Québec.

CRREL. The following booklets were published by CRREL (the Cold Regions Research & Engineering Laboratory) in Hanover, New Hampshire:

Clark, Elmer F. "Camp Century." Technical report 174, October 1965.

Mellor, Malcolm. "Methods of Building on Permanent Snowfields." Monograph III-A2a, October 1968.

Mellor, Malcolm. "Investigation and Exploitation of Snow Field Sites." Monograph III-A2b, January 1969.

Curtiss, Mina. *A Forgotten Empress: Anna Ivanovna and Her Era*. Frederick Ungar Publishing Company, New York.

The Daily Mail and Empire, Toronto, Canada (January 24, 1922–January 31, 1922).

Daily Mercury, Québec (January 16, 1894–February 3, 1894; January 11, 1896–January 29, 1896).

Daily News, St. Paul, Minnesota (January 15, 1938).

Dawson, Samuel Edward. *Montreal Winter Carnival, 1884*. Supplement to *Dawson's Hand-book* for the City of Montreal.

L'Evenement Journal, Québec (January 5, 1955–February 1, 1955).

Fisher, Thomas. "Cold Calculations," *Progressive Architecture* (November 1982), pp. 134–139.

The Gazette, Montreal (January 1, 1884–February 7, 1884; January 29, 1894–February 5, 1894; January 27, 1896–February 1, 1896; January 25, 1909–February 20, 1909; January 25, 1910–February 9, 1910; January 20, 1922–January 31, 1922).

Government of Ontario, Ministry of Tourism and Recreation. "Ontario/Canada Traveller's Encyclopaedia."

Harvey, Mrs. James R. "The Leadville Ice Palace of 1896." *Colorado Magazine* (May 1940), pp. 94–101.

Horizon Magazine Editors. *The Horizon History of Russia*. American Heritage Publishing Company (1970), p. 190.

Japan National Tourist Organization brochures:
"Northern Japan: Hokkaido and Tohoku."
"Hokkaido."

Kaufman, Michael T. "What's Doing in Québec City." *The New York Times*, Sunday, January 23, 1983, Travel Section, p. 10.

Kingery, W. D., ed. *Ice and Snow*, The M.I.T. Press, Cambridge, Mass., 1963.

Krafft, George Wolffgang. *Description et Représentation Exacte de la Maison de Glace, construite à St. Petersbourg au mois de Janvier 1740*. Translated from the German by Pierre Louis LeRoy. St. Petersburg, 1741.

The Leadville Crystal Carnival Association. "Leadville Crystal Carnival." Leadville, Colorado, January 1896.

Lipsey, John J. "When Leadville Built a Palace of Ice." *Week End*, March 1, 1957.

Longwell, D. "The Leadville Ice Palace." May 15, 1968. (Unpublished paper, in the Leadville Public Library).

Mellor, Malcolm. "A Review of Basic Snow Mechanics." *Snow Mechanics* (Proceedings of the Grindelwald Symposium, April 1974) IAHS-AISH Publ. No. 114, 1975.

Miyazawa, Eiji (Black Star). "Snow Festival in Japan's Far North." *National Geographic*, Vol. 134, No. 6 (December 1968), pp. 824-833.

Montreal Star (1884 Carnival Number; 1887 Carnival Number).

Montreal Witness (1885 Carnival Number; 1887 Carnival Number; February 11, 1909; January 14, 1910).

The New York Times (January 27, 1885–January 28, 1885; January 12, 1886; January 22, 1887–February 13, 1887; January 18, 1895–January 26, 1895).

The Northwest Illustrated Monthly Magazine, Vol. VI, No. 2 (February 1888), pp. 1–5.

O'Keefe & Stockdorf, Official Photographers for the Ice Palace Association, 1896. (Document in the library, State Historical Society of Colorado.)

Olsen, Robert Arthur. "A History of the Saint Paul Ice Palaces."

The Ottawa Citizen (February 4, 1904; February 4, 1922).

The Ottawa Journal (December 27, 1894–January 26, 1895; January 25, 1922–February 4, 1922).

Perutz, Dr. M. F. "The Bergship Plan." *Penguin Science News IX*, pp. 131–141.

Quebec Chronicle-Telegraph (January 11, 1962–February 27, 1962).

Ralph, Julian. Article in *Montreal Star* (1887 Carnival Number).

Sapporo Snow Festival brochures: "The 33rd Sapporo Snow Festival."

"Sapporo Snow Festival."

Smith, Clyde H. "How to Build an Igloo," *Country Journal*, Vol. IV, No. 1 (January 1977).

Le Soleil, Quebec (January 15, 1956–January 30, 1956; January 8, 1957–January 29, 1957; January 13, 1965–February 13, 1965; January 12, 1966–February 15, 1966; January 25, 1967–January 27, 1967; February 5, 1969–February 14, 1969; January 17, 1974–February 15, 1974).

St. Paul Dispatch (December 20, 1887–January 25, 1888; October 12, 1895–January 18, 1896; January 15, 1938–January 26, 1938).

St. Paul Pioneer Press (December 20, 1887–January 26, 1888; January 5, 1896–January 22, 1896; January 25, 1937–February 7, 1937; January 23, 1938–January 31, 1938; January 8, 1940–January 28, 1940; January 11, 1941–February 14, 1941; January 18, 1942–February 2, 1942; January 19, 1947–February 10, 1947).

St. Paul Winter Carnival Association publications: "The Crystal Carnival," 1886.

"History, St. Paul Winter Carnival."

"Saint Paul Winter Carnival Souvenir Booklet, 1886–1961."

"St. Paul Ice Palace Illustrated," 1886–1887.

"St. Paul Winter Carnival," 1896.

"St. Paul's First Winter Carnival," *Brick Pomeroy's Democrat* (1886).

West and Call, St. Paul, Minnesota, January 18, 1938.

Wildman, Edwin. "The Passing of the Ice Carnival." *Outing* (January 1899), pp. 360–363.

Picture Credits

(Numbers refer to page)

Anderes/Agranoff Collection: 55, top right; 124, top and bottom; 125. Archives de la Ville de Québec, Centre de documentation photographique: 71. Archives Nationales du Québec: 68, top and bottom right, collection J. E. Livernois; 72, collection Initiale. Archives Nationales du Québec, collection Fonds Carnaval de Québec, MS 1894: 38, left and right; 39; 69. Bibliothèque Nationale, Gouvernement du Québec, Ministère des Affaires Culturelles: 19; 20; 27; 33, left; 35; 37, bottom left. British Museum: 7. Carnaval de Québec: 114; 115; 116; 117. Colorado Historical Society: 78, William H. Jackson; 82. CRREL (U. S. Army Cold Regions Research and Engineering Laboratory): 17; 121. Denver Public Library: 80, left and right; 83, William H. Jackson. Ken L. Elder Collection: 44; 45; 77. Hidezo Imaruoka: cover; frontispiece; 106; 107; 108; 110; 111; 112. McCord Museum, McGill University: 24; 38, center; 40. McGill University Libraries: 22; 33, right; 36. Minnesota Historical Society: 6; 8; 10, T. W. Ingersoll; 18, top and bottom; 46, H. Brosius; 48, left and right; 49, top left and right, bottom right, Zimmerman and Ingersoll; 50, T. W. Ingersoll; 51, C. A. Zimmerman; 52, H. H. Bennett; 53, left, C. A. Zimmerman, right, C. J. Greenleaf; 54; 55, top center, bottom, H. Brosius; 56, Ingersoll and Zimmerman; 57; 58, T. W. Ingersoll; 59; 60; 61, upper left and right, lower right, H. H. Bennett; 62; 63, left and right; 64; 65, top and bottom; 66, C. P. Gibson; 84, top; 87; 91; 93, bottom, Larry Schreiber; 96; 97. Ville de Montréal, Division des Archives: 28, left. National Library of Canada: 21; 28, right; 74, left. New York Public Library, The Astor, Lenox, and Tilden Foundations, Art, Prints, and Photographs Division: 12; 14; 15. New York Society Library: 25; 27; 68. Notman Photographic Archives, McCord Museum: 26, William Notman; 29, William Notman; 30, William Notman; 31, William Notman; 32, William Notman; 37, top right, William Notman, bottom right; 43. Frei Otto: 122, copyright 1962. Public Archives Canada: 9; 42; 70; 74. Rafferty, Rafferty, Mikutowski, Roney, Architects: 102, bottom; 103. Saint Paul, Minnesota, Division of Parks & Recreation (Gary Mortensen, photographer): 88; 89; 90; 93, top; 94; 95; 98; 99; 100; 101. Saint Paul Winter Carnival Association: 84, bottom; 92; 102, top. Uni Photo (Japan): 118, Osamu Mizuno.

Index

(Figures in *italics* are illustrations)

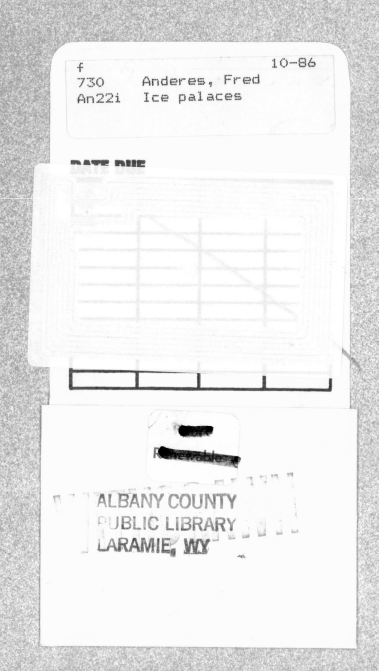